FIGHT THEM FOR THE BEECHES

A comedy drama by

Kathy Reid

Acknowledgements
Many thanks to Marc Reid and Paula Montie for their great ideas and unwavering support without which my fight to create The Beeches would have never been won!

CHARACTERS

Lord Christopher Cornwallis becomes the owner of The Beeches Manor House including the residential home. He is vain, proud and hides his empathic side well.

Lady Caroline Cornwallis The kindly and seemingly rather frail mother of Cornwallis.

Sam Harris Home Manager of The Beeches who is professional, efficient, organised and always wants to do 'the right thing'.

Honey Potter Chef and General Assistant of The Beeches Residential Home who is caring and kind.

The Colonel Resident of Room 1 who after his experience of war is commanding, instructive and still has a lot of fight in him.

Walker Resident of Room 2 who knows everything and everybody and is always in the middle of a deal.

George Resident of Room 3 who is new to the home as a vacancy was created on the death of Cecil (a good friend of the other residents) and is quiet and secretive.

Iris Resident of Room 4 who is intelligent and private with a love of words and crosswords.

Cassandra Aka Woo Woo. Resident of Room 5 who is colourful, larger than life and spiritually connected.

The first performance of Fight Them For The Beeches was given on 11th May 2023 by Twyford Drama at Loddon Hall, Twyford, with the following cast:

Lord Christopher Cornwallis	Marc Reid
Lady Caroline Cornwallis	Hazel Evans
Sam Harris	Jac Rampton
Honey Potter	Sam Gittins
The Colonel	Richard Rudman
Walker	Mike Higgins
George	Ian McDonald
Iris	Katherine Lewis
Cassandra	Rebecca Down

ACT ONE

SCENE ONE

Forest Lounge of the Residential Home of The Beeches Manor which is grand but faded and rather shabbily furnished with a portrait of Lord John Cornwallis on the wall. Enter Sam who has called an early morning meeting and Honey who will busily and cheerily hand out coffee to the assembled residents.

HONEY	Good luck.
SAM	Thanks.
HONEY	You look ever so pale.

Sam shrugs.

HONEY	Whatever it is, it'll be fine.
SAM	I'm sworn to secrecy.
HONEY	I understand.
SAM	Sorry.
HONEY	It'll be fine.

Sam turns away to look up at the portrait. Enter residents who complain how early it is. Colonel walks with an exaggerated swagger, looking at his watch and muttering loudly about the time, Cassandra wafts around 'sensing the early morning energies' and then meditating, Walker is texting, Iris is slow but very businesslike as she sorts crossword books by her chair and George looks lost, sits in the wrong chair and is told to move. All eventually sit in 'their' chairs.

COLONEL	We'd barely finished breakfast.
SAM	Sorry.
COLONEL	Coffee. Forest Lounge 10.30. On the dot. And certainly not 9.22.
SAM	Sorry.
COLONEL	What the dickens is going on?
WALKER	(*to Sam*) Cheer up. You look like somebody's died.

Awkward pause.

SAM	The owner wants to talk to you all.
COLONEL	What about?

WALKER	Lord John's coming 'ere?
COLONEL	He's back on his feet?
CASSANDRA	A miracle, a wondrous miracle.
SAM	The owner will explain.
COLONEL	Iris, he's talking in riddles. That's your department.
IRIS	A riddle soon to be solved Colonel. It isn't difficult to answer this one I'm afraid.
COLONEL	Give us a clue then.
IRIS	Seven letters 'Going by into God's acre'.
COLONEL	Going by into God's acre.
IRIS	Anybody?

All mumble and shrug shoulders.

IRIS	The answer is obvious. It's 'Passing'.
COLONEL	You're going to have to explain that one Iris.
IRIS	Going by is passing and into God's Acre is going into a Churchyard so passing as in dying.
COLONEL	Right?
CASSANDRA	That one was hard Iris. Why did you choose that?
IRIS	You're the psychic.

Cassandra stops to concentrate on what Iris has said.

COLONEL	Too hard for 9.23 am!
GEORGE	Is this normal for a Tuesday morning?
CASSANDRA	Iris is right. Something's up. How did I miss it? Look at Sam's energy.

George approaches Sam and looks him up and down. Sam has his head buried in paperwork.

GEORGE	His what?
CASSANDRA	His energy. Look about him. The colour is very dark. It feels heavy. Sam's being is literally under a cloud.

GEORGE   Dark? No. Heavy? No. No cloud either. *(aside)* Only cloud cuckoo land. *(to Iris)* There is no scientific evidence for....

IRIS   Cassandra has the gift. However, you don't need the gift to know what's going on today.

George looks clueless.

GEORGE   Let's look at the facts.

CASSANDRA   Wait...

George jumps out of his skin and is affronted.

CASSANDRA   Cornwallis will come here with very bad news.

COLONEL   Good chap. Haven't seen John in ages.

Cassandra makes a big display of focusing on her premonition.

CASSANDRA   It's not clear. I'm getting Lord Cornwallis but it's not him.

GEORGE   Hold on! Let me get this straight. You're saying you can tell who's coming through that door and what they're going to say? Prove it.

CASSANDRA   *(to herself)* No, I don't understand. Need to focus.

Cassandra goes into a trance and moves away from George.

GEORGE   Typical. As soon as you ask for proof, there's nothing. It's all fantasy.

IRIS   *(to George)* You'll have your proof just wait.

Sam is silent and pacing by the door. Walker approaches Sam.

WALKER   'Ere mate, what's the deal?

Silence.

WALKER   What's going down?

Silence.

WALKER   Come on Sam, time's precious. Less time, less deals. Time is...

COLONEL   Money. We know! We've heard it often enough!

IRIS   Only ten times a day!

CASSANDRA   *(to Walker distractedly)* Move beyond the material into the realms of the eternal.

WALKER   I like the material. Feel that.

Walker holds out his clothing to Cassandra.

CASSANDRA   Walker. You are impossible. Let me focus.

GEORGE   Bonkers.

Cassandra nudges Walker, points to Sam and sits to meditate.

WALKER   Looks like Sam needs a drink?

Walker opens a secret stash and pulls out a bottle of whisky.

SAM   I'm on duty. I didn't see that.

WALKER   See what?

SAM   Exactly.

WALKER   Tell us the scoop.

SAM   Can't say.

COLONEL   Can't or won't?

SAM   Just can't.

WALKER   Yes you can!

Honey pushes the tea trolley / tray into Walker.

HONEY   Oops, pardon me Walker. Coffee?

Sam shoots Honey a smile of gratitude.

WALKER   Ta.

HONEY   *(to Walker)* We'll find out soon enough.

Honey carefully guides Walker away from Sam.

WALKER   *(winking lasciviously)* Aye, aye. Somethin' good is it?

HONEY   I really don't know.

COLONEL   *(getting up)* Can't or won't Sam?

SAM   Not now Colonel.

COLONEL   As good a time as any.

Honey swiftly moves across to The Colonel and lightly pushes him back into his chair.

HONEY   Sit Colonel. Do make yourself comfortable. I could rustle up your favourite coffee. Shall I?

COLONEL   *(excited)* A Masters?

HONEY	One Master's Mochaccino coming up.
COLONEL	Right on. And it's not even a Bank Holiday.
HONEY	Cassandra can you do the usual?

Honey rushes back to the tea trolley, where Cassandra, still in a trance, shakes a flask and waves her hand over it then pours the contents into a cup onto which Honey squirts cream and crumbles a flake.

COLONEL	With cream?
HONEY	With extra cream Colonel.
COLONEL	And....
HONEY	Chocolate shavings!
CASSANDRA	Whole slabs of choc... (*silence*)... Take care. Bad news is ahead. Not just today. More is circling around us.
IRIS	Fatally bad.
COLONEL	Can you give me that clue again Iris?

Iris is unimpressed. Honey helps before Iris loses her temper.

HONEY	Here, your Master.
COLONEL	Love it when you say that. Got to stick to the old routines. There'd be chaos otherwise. Boy, that hits the spot.

The Colonel becomes lost in his coffee and forgets the clue. He gets cream on his face.

CASSANDRA	*(to Iris)* You felt something bad coming too?
IRIS	Felt? No. Worked it out. Plain as the cream on his face.

Cassandra and Iris laugh.

WALKER	*(taking the mick)* I feel it.
CASSANDRA	Then it must be bad.
GEORGE	*(aside)* Tosh! I've landed in a mad house.

Noise near the door. Sam coughs. All stop.

COLONEL	Positions everybody.
SAM	Behave! All of you. Please.
COLONEL	*(indignant)* Of course.

WALKER   Why wouldn't we?

CASSANDRA   Naturally.

CORNWALLIS *(off)* Sam!

IRIS   As always.

SAM   I'll be straight back.

Sam exits anxiously.

WALKER   That's a threat. 'Ere, while the cat's away...

Walker opens another secret stash and takes out a small whisky bottle.

WALKER   Did a deal on this great malt. Comes from a class distillery in the Outer Hebrides - dark, peaty.... Anybody?

Everybody nods except Colonel. Walker dishes it out.

COLONEL   Incorrigible.

IRIS   Think we'll need this.

CASSANDRA   Love a good earthy malt.

GEORGE   Mine's a double.

Walker goes to put the bottle away.

COLONEL   Don't miss me man.

Cassandra sips her whisky and then stops in her tracks.

CASSANDRA   No!

George particularly jumps out of his skin.

GEORGE   *(to Cassandra)* No need to add to the drama.

CASSANDRA   It's the worst news.

IRIS   *(aside)* You're only just catching up with me!

Sam enters and opens the door to Cornwallis who enters dressed in mourning suit and black tie and confidently stands before residents.

SAM   *(stresses the title)* Lord Christopher Cornwallis.

COLONEL   Lord....He can't be.

CASSANDRA   He is.

GEORGE   No!

IRIS	God bless Lord Cornwallis. *(aside)* He has passed. I knew it.
WALKER	'E can't leave us.
HONEY	*(loudly)* He can't be .... I saw him last night. He was in great spirits.
CASSANDRA	And now at peace with the spirits.

Honey rushes out in tears. Sam turns to Cornwallis.

SAM	Might I leave?
CORNWALLIS	You're needed here.
GEORGE	*(aside)* We're in for it now. So is the Manor. You don't need psychic powers to know that. Christopher Cornwallis will not be the same Lord as his father.
WALKER	*(loudly)* Well informed, aint you George? Seeing as you've only lived 'ere five minutes.
GEORGE	*(hesitant)* Well, um, it's obvious.

Cornwallis looks down his nose at George clearly not knowing who he is and clears his throat proprietorially.

SAM	Quiet everybody, please. There's an important announcement.
CORNWALLIS	I am the bearer of sad news. *(coughs)* Very sad news. It is incumbent upon me to inform you all that Lord John Cornwallis passed away in his sleep last night. His passing was mercifully peaceful. God rest your soul Father.
COLONEL	Yes, God rest Lord Cornwallis' soul.
ALL	God rest Lord Cornwallis' soul.

One by one Colonel, Walker, Cassandra and Iris stand, place one arm across their chest, bow their heads to the portrait.

IRIS	To The Boss.
COL/W/CAS	The Boss.

Pause with few sobs and tears including from Cornwallis.

CORNWALLIS	I know this will hit you all hard. The City has taken so much of my time in recent years and I haven't been able to visit my dear father as often as I would have liked.

WALKER	*(aside)* Never saw you.
GEORGE	*(aside)* You never liked the manor.
CORNWALLIS	However, I do know how highly he respected you all. God rest your soul Father.
COLONEL	Yes God rest Lord Cornwallis' soul.

All residents whisper the same. Cornwallis stands back nods at Sam who moves forward.

SAM	We are now privileged to call you Lord Cornwallis of Beeches Manor Estate.

George collapses into a chair. Silence.

IRIS	How will you manage the estate?
CASSANDRA	Iris! It's too soon.
CORNWALLIS	As Lord of this estate I will continue my father's legacy.
COLONEL	We're very pleased to hear that.
IRIS	When will Lord Cornwallis be laid to rest?
CORNWALLIS	You will be informed in due course.
SAM	I'll let everybody know as soon as possible.
CASSANDRA	Thank you. I'm sure we all wish to attend.
IRIS	How is Lady Cornwallis?
CORNWALLIS	Mother is fine.
COLONEL	Fine? She'll be devastated.
IRIS	Is she well? We haven't seen her in such a long time.
WALKER	Lord and Lady Cornwallis loved coming 'ere for a good old chat.
COLONEL	Lady C's not been here since The Boss became ill.
IRIS	When can we give Lady Cornwallis our condolences?
CORNWALLIS	In due course. My first priority is the welfare of my darling Mama. Thank you again for your kind words and condolences. I will pass these all on to Mama.
COLONEL	This is a sad, dark day.

CORNWALLIS So much sadder and darker to his family don't you think. I must leave. There is a great deal to organise.

Awkward pause. Cornwallis turns to exit.

SAM Thank you for coming to tell us Sir. We appreciate Lord Cornwallis taking the trouble at this difficult time. Don't we everybody?

ALL *(mumble)* Thank you.

Cornwallis nods and exits.

SAM I know you will all be very upset at this tragic news. We all loved Lord John. Such a fine man. His legacy lives on in every stone of this manor. Lord Christopher Cornwallis assured us he will continue running the estate just like his father.

GEORGE *(to himself)* Sure.

COLONEL That is one blessing. None of us are up for change in any shape. We all have a long association to this house. Apart from George of course.

GEORGE What do you mean? I...

COLONEL You're new here.

GEORGE Yes of course.

SAM I must go and find Honey. Check she's okay.

WALKER Go comfort 'er Sam.

SAM As her manager I will check that she is fit to carry on her duties. If that's alright with you Walker?

WALKER Course. I'm sure you'll comfort 'er well.

Sam is annoyed and exits.

SCENE TWO

The same. Following.

CASSANDRA You can't help yourself can you?

WALKER I am what I am.

COLONEL As subtle as a V2 rocket.

WALKER	Just telling it like it is.
CASSANDRA	Feel the room and you will sense when to stop.
IRIS	Even I know when to stop!

Iris looks around at the disbelieving faces.

COLONEL	When's the funeral, how will you manage the estate, can we see Lady Cornwallis?
IRIS	They're only questions. Questions that need answers.
GEORGE	We need answers. Don't just believe what you're told. Dig, dig, dig that's what must be done. Unless of course Cassandra already has the answers.

Everybody ignores George's weird behaviour.

IRIS	You still don't believe in her. Even when she...
GEORGE	*(dismissively)* No. It's fantasy.
CASSANDRA	*(to distract)* The year 2000 is clearly a time of challenge. First Cecil and now The Boss pass to the other side. *(speaks to heavens)* We will miss you Lord John Cornwallis. And not only those delicious treats and great stories you used to bring us. We will miss your kind spirit. You are such a loving soul. A true gentleman.
WALKER	Could The Boss spin a tale! 'Ilarious. Generous to a fault too. Specially with the old *(whistles and mimics pouring a drink)* . No alcohol ban in BS days.
COLONEL	Thick chocolate biscuits in BS days.
CASSANDRA	Scented candles in BS days.
IRIS	All the dailies free too.
GEORGE	BS days?
COLONEL	Yes BS. Halcyon days.
GEORGE	What?
IRIS	BS. Before Stroke.
COLONEL	The stroke changed him.
CASSANDRA	Never came to see us after that. BS he'd be here nearly every day.

Cassandra sobs and Iris comforts her in an unemotional way.

COLONEL   The stroke clearly affected his mind and his personality.

GEORGE   I don't think so.

COLONEL   How would you know? You weren't here! BS he would never have slashed the food budget, closed the swimming pool and cut the flowers, the Christmas decorations, the parties and even our weekly trips out.

Colonel points at Millennium decorations.

COLONEL   We even had to pay for that ourselves and that's why it's not coming down for a very long time.

GEORGE   I don't believe you. Lord Cornwallis was no ... I can't believe ....he was a penny pincher.

COLONEL   Are you calling me a liar?

CASSANDRA   It was the stroke George. Lord John was a very generous man.

GEORGE   BS?

CASSANDRA   Yes.

WALKER   Life got 'arder.

IRIS   AS.

GEORGE   After Stroke?

IRIS   Yes. AS it is all about the finances.

GEORGE   *(aside)* I wonder why?

WALKER   Could 'ave sorted out deals on food, trips, anythin, but 'e was never interested.

COLONEL   You got to talk to The Boss?

WALKER   No, only Sam...'Ey, do you think Sam was cuttin' the budget and pocketin' the difference?

CASSANDRA   Our Sam? Committing fraud? How funny.

All laugh.

COLONEL   Today's not funny though is it?

CASSANDRA   No, we've lost the best of men. To The Boss.

All, except George, stand and face the portrait, bowing their heads with their hands across the chest.

ALL	The Boss.
WALKER	Good to 'ear 'is son will carry it all on.
COLONEL	Maintain the course. That's the spirit.
CASSANDRA	The spirit wasn't there. His words on his father and mother were heartfelt but I didn't get the same feeling when he talked about the legacy...
COLONEL	Woo Woo hold the feelings. There's enough emotion flying around today as it is. I'm exhausted.
IRIS	Good point.
COLONEL	What point Iris?
IRIS	I've read between the lines Colonel. You're saying we're all tired and could do with a rest.
COLONEL	You're spot on. You deduced that before I knew it myself. Time for a rest and reflect troops.

All rise to leave.

GEORGE	Why does he call you Woo Woo?
CASSANDRA	Isn't it obvious?
GEORGE	I haven't seen anything out of the ordinary.
CASSANDRA	No?
IRIS	You don't think Cassandra sensed the news before Cornwallis entered the room.
GEORGE	I saw no substance to that. I'm a man of science, cold hard facts not all this airy fairy, weirdy, other wordly stuff.
CASSANDRA	Really?
GEORGE	If you can't see it, touch it, hear it, taste it or smell it then it doesn't exist.
WALKER	*(to George)* 'Lectricity?
GEORGE	*(to Walker)* You can prove that exists. You can't prove the existence of any of this extrasensory stuff.
CASSANDRA	Is that so?

Cassandra waves her arms around.

GEORGE   There is no scientific basis....

George is frozen.

CASSANDRA   Perhaps science is too limited to prove the "extrasensory stuff".

Cassandra waves her arms around.

GEORGE   .... to prove anything that...

George stops and looks puzzled and confused. All laugh.

CASSANDRA   You're right George.

COLONEL   Lesson over. Time to rest and reflect.

WALKER   If we're reflectin' then...

Walker opens a cupboard and takes out some brandy.

WALKER   You're welcome to join me.

CASSANDRA   You'll pickle your brain.

WALKER   I'd "relish" that! See what I did there Iris?

IRIS   Congratulations Walker. Don't you have some deal to be sorting out?

WALKER   Always. I'll just do a quick inventory.

All exit except George and Walker who checks a few stashes around the room. George stares up at the portrait/photo of Lord John Cornwallis and bows his head. Thinking he's alone George takes out his phone and Walker listens.

GEORGE   James, it's me. You've heard the news from Beeches Manor? Thank you. Very sad day for us all. Thought you would know. Your ear is so close to the ground it's in Australia. First step, Newfield Housing. Set the wheels in motion now. Good. No I'm fine thanks, *(emotion building)* got to keep strong, especially now. Nobody suspects a thing. Got to make sure it stays that way too. Keep me posted.

George exits. Lights down.

SCENE THREE

Morning. Lights up. Cleaning cupboard with cleaning products and two makeshift stools side by side. Enter Honey who collapses onto a stool in despair and looks to the heavens.

HONEY   Sorry. I didn't do enough. I should have helped you more. Never knew you were so ill.

Enter Sam

SAM   Neither did I.

HONEY   Sam!

SAM   Didn't mean to make you jump. How are you?

HONEY   Okay.

SAM   You're not okay.

HONEY   I am.

SAM   You don't look okay.

HONEY   Yes I do.

SAM   You're all wound up.

HONEY   No I'm not.

SAM   Of course you are. The news about Lord John. Sorry I couldn't prepare you. Are you cross?

HONEY   No.

SAM   You're not cross with me?

HONEY   Why would I be?

SAM   I'd understand if you were.

HONEY   Well I'm not.

SAM   Good.

HONEY   Good.

Honey shrugs. Sam goes to touch her shoulder but doesn't dare.

SAM   I know it's difficult.

HONEY   Such a lovely man. Always interested in me and everybody here. So kind, so generous....

SAM   I know.

HONEY   Did you know he was that ill?

SAM   No. I'm still in shock.

HONEY	We should have worked things out when Christopher arrived. Barely seen him before.
SAM	Don't call him that.
HONEY	That's his name. Christopher Cornwallis.
SAM	He's Lord Cornwallis. We must respect that.
HONEY	Even here?
SAM	Yes.
HONEY	What's got into you?
SAM	We need to adjust to the new.
HONEY	If you say so. *(awkward pause)* Do you know much about him?
SAM	Chris...Lord Cornwallis?
HONEY	It's strange that he never really visited his aging parents or helped them run this huge estate.
SAM	That's not for us to judge.
HONEY	What has got into you?
SAM	I'm tired.
HONEY	Of course. Today must be gruelling for you. You're having to think of us all.

Honey puts her hand on Sam's knee which he ignores.

SAM	This is what I think. Lord Cornwallis is a decent man and will continue his father's legacy. In our roles as Manager and General Assistant we must give him all the support he needs. Agreed.

Sam stands and Honey's hand falls to the ground.

HONEY	*(subdued)* Agreed.
SAM	Just came to see that you were okay.

Honey stands and goes to hug Sam.

HONEY	I'm fine. How are you?
SAM	Must dash. Lots to do. *(seeing Honey's face)* I will see you later. We can chat more then. Bye.
HONEY	*(perplexed)* Bye.

Lights down.

SCENE FOUR

Lights up. Five days later. Midday. Sound of funeral church bells. Enter Colonel, Cassandra, Iris and Walker into the Forest Lounge dressed in black and grieving.

COLONEL	*(collapsing into his chair)* A fine service and a good spread. Honey ... excelled herself.
WALKER	Apart from marmite and tuna sandwiches. Yuck.
IRIS	And burnt vol au vents. Most unlike her.
COLONEL	I was being polite.
CASSANDRA	She's very stressed.
IRIS	She was very fond of Lord John.
CASSANDRA	Of course.
WALKER	Not as fond as she is of Sam.
CASSANDRA	Stop that Walker. We don't want to upset her.
WALKER	Sam can comfort 'er then, can't 'e Colonel?
COLONEL	Cut it out.
WALKER	Sam, comfort Honey, know what I mean?
COLONEL	I said cut it out.

Walker opens his mouth.

COLONEL	Now!

Walker closes his mouth.

WALKER	Permission to speak.
COLONEL	Is it to do with Honey or Sam?
WALKER	No. George.
CASSANDRA	George? Unexpected.
WALKER	After all these years I can still surprise you.
COLONEL	Get on with it Walker.
WALKER	Today might not be a good day, but I've got to get this off me chest.
COLONEL	I said get on with it.

WALKER   George was on his teeny, tiny mobile phone....it fits in his top pocket... must have cost a fortune. Mine's the size of a wardrobe.

Walker mimes taking a call on his enormous phone.

COLONEL   Get to the point man.

WALKER   George was tellin' somebody to contact Newfield Housin'.

Iris immediately gets out a laptop from under her chair.

IRIS   Newfield Housing? Are you sure? They've had their eyes on the estate for years.

WALKER   Definitely said Newfield. What the 'eck is that?

IRIS   A Sony Vaio laptop Walker.

WALKER   New?

IRIS   Of course.

WALKER   Wow. What did you pay for that?

IRIS   Pay? I still have contacts you know.

WALKER   I 'umbly apologise for suggestin' you'd dirty you 'ands with cash, Your Greatness.

Walker bows before Iris, George ambles in. Iris hides laptop.

GEORGE   More drama?

WALKER   No drama 'ere.

COLONEL   Good. We should be paying tribute to Lord John. The Boss. Our friend, landlord and leader through many battles.

GEORGE   Battles?

Iris shoots a dark look at Colonel.

IRIS   Fights to keep his house and our home. Beeches Manor is in our blood and where we all want to live until the end. We will continue to fight for that, won't we Colonel.

COLONEL   *(catching on)* Yes of course.

GEORGE   *(bemused)* What fights?

IRIS   First, dry rot which you spotted Colonel.

COLONEL   Military training you see. Eyes like a hawk. Nose like a bloodhound. Ears like a bat.

GEORGE   *(low)* Head the size of an elephant.

COLONEL   What's that?

GEORGE   Nothing.

CASSANDRA   Then the plan for the high speed rail link straight through the grounds.

COLONEL   We kept that at bay.

WALKER   Cecil paid for those emergency repairs to the roof. Bloomin' Council wanted to close us down for 'ealth and safety.

COLONEL   We weren't going to let some holes in the roof get in our way.

GEORGE   Cecil?

CASSANDRA   You've taken over his room?

GEORGE   Right. How could I forget? *(low)* Saint Cecil.

WALKER   Can I see the new phone.

GEORGE   New phone?

WALKER   The tiny phone that sits in your pocket just there.

GEORGE   No time. Must go.

George can't escape as the residents gather round George.

WALKER   Who've you been phonin' on that tiny, tiny phone George?

COLONEL   Who've you been meeting in town George?

CASSANDRA   Your aura is very red George. Are you stressed?

CASSANDRA

Cassandra pushes George into a chair.

IRIS   Why can't I find any record of a George Lowe of your age? Is George Lowe really your name?

George stands.

GEORGE   Don't be ridiculous. Leave me alone. You're all mad.

George exits.

COLONEL	We're mad angry. How could Cecil leave us with a fraudster? Cecil we miss you.
IRIS	Cecil was like a brother to me.
COLONEL	We're losing all the good ones.
WALKER	I'm still 'ere.

Everybody laughs.

WALKER	What's funny?
CASSANDRA	Nothing Walker.

Honey enters with coffee.

COLONEL	Ah coffee. Nice idea Honey.
HONEY	Thank you Colonel. Thought you might need an extra cup today.
IRIS	Do you know why Lady C didn't go to the funeral Honey?
CASSANDRA	Iris please!
HONEY	Haven't seen her since Lord John... she needs space to grieve. I've been leaving her meals outside her door. I'm sure things will get back to normal soon.
COLONEL	This place is best when we all follow the rules of the day.
HONEY	I love this place too Colonel and this job with all of you.
CASSANDRA	Thank you Honey. We love you too!
IRIS	You're special to us.
COLONEL	Here, here,

Pause. Walker approaches Honey boldly.

WALKER	What's Sam's game 'oney?
HONEY	Wh...what?
WALKER	Sam's game. With Cornwallis? He's become a total Yes Man.

Walker does an impression of Sam.

WALKER	Yes Lord Cornwallis, of course my Lord, certainly, right away.

Awkward pause.

WALKER	What's goin' on?
HONEY	You're all looking at me.
WALKER	What's the deal?
HONEY	I don't know. Why would I know?
WALKER	*(raising eyebrows)* You must know the score.
HONEY	I don't.
WALKER	Yeah you do.
HONEY	I'm only the assistant. They don't discuss things with me. How am I meant to know?
WALKER	You and Sam. You're....
CASSANDRA	Walker, enough.
WALKER	...close.
HONEY	I don't know what you're going on about.

Honey turns to leave as Sam enters. They bump into each other and are embarrassed.

CASSANDRA	Honey, we're sorry, come back.

Cassandra encourages Sam to follow Honey to the door. Sam opens the door for her as she exits with the coffee.

COLONEL	Come back. We need our coffee.
CASSANDRA	You're addicted to caffeine Colonel.
IRIS	*(low)* Long term analysis of non-verbal behaviour indicates Honey and Sam are in four letter word beginning with L. The clue is...
WALKER	*(loudly)* Lust! *(low)* Way hay.
CASSANDRA	You're addicted to innuendo Walker.
COLONEL	Where's your decorum man? Things are descending into chaos.
WALKER	With a capital K.
IRIS	Walker, really!

Sam is back from opening the door for Honey.

SAM	*(corporate)* Can I have your attention please.
COLONEL	What now?

SAM	Lord Christopher Cornwallis is calling a meeting for 4pm.

All moan and groan.

COLONEL	Tea time.
SAM	Here in the Forest Lounge.
IRIS	And the reason for this honour?
SAM	I can't say.
WALKER	Not again.
COLONEL	Can't or won't say Sam?
SAM	I just can't say.
IRIS	Let's focus on what Sam can say shall we?
SAM	Thank you Iris. Sound advice. I've got to go to a meeting. Sorry. We'll all find out more soon.
CASSANDRA	From Cornwallis?
SAM	Yes.
CASSANDRA	On the day of his father's funeral?
SAM	Yes.
CASSANDRA	Oh dear!

Cassandra faints into a chair and all surround her.

COLONEL	It's okay Sam, she's coming round. You go off to your meeting. We'll let you know if there's any problem.

Sam exits.

WALKER	He's gone Cass.
COLONEL	What is it Woo Woo, what did you see?

Cassandra is back to normal.

CASSANDRA	Something bad, not sure what.
IRIS	Tell us more.
CASSANDRA	I need to go to my room.
COLONEL	A lie down. Good idea. It's an emotion ... difficult day.
IRIS	Time for a rest everybody.

All exit. Lights down.

SCENE FIVE

Lights up. Small dark room in the manor house. Grieving Lady Cornwallis sits in an armchair by a table with a glass of water and bottle of pills. Enter Cornwallis with a small plate of food.

CORNWALLIS *(unemotional)* Such a moving ceremony. Reverend Green did an excellent job. The Lord Lieutenant's words were so kind and The Mayor brought us all to tears. The residents insisted on speaking as well and said such touching even loving things about The Boss as they call him.

LADY C Wonderful.

CORNWALLIS You look cold. Let me put this over you. Are you comfortable?

LADY C Thank you.

CORNWALLIS The number of bouquets was incredible. All with such touching sentiments. Father made an incredible impact on those around him.

LADY C I know.

CORNWALLIS You look tired. Just as well you didn't attend. It would have been too much.

Lady C turns away in emotional pain.

CORNWALLIS Yes. Too much. We need to take care of you now. You are the priority.

LADY C How kind.

CORNWALLIS We need to keep you strong and in good health.

Lady C sobs. She cannot speak or move.

CORNWALLIS Hush. We must hold it together. That's what father would have wanted. All day I've put my feelings aside to venerate him. My whole life has been serving others and putting my needs aside in preparation for this weighty role which I now shoulder. As his first born and only child I undertake this role in his honour. That's the way it should be isn't it? *(pause)* I will leave you in peace to eat. Don't forget to take your pills. They will help. Bye mother.

Cornwallis kisses his hand and places it on his mother's forehead swiftly. Cornwallis exits. Lights down.

SCENE SIX

Lights up. Forest Lounge 4pm that afternoon. All residents are sat for afternoon tea which Honey serves. All look sad.

IRIS For her not to have made the funeral, Lady C must be very ill.

CASSANDRA It is worrying.

IRIS What sense do you get of her?

Cassandra goes into a meditative state.

CASSANDRA Dark, sorrowful, contained. But mainly there's this darkness.

IRIS That is all to be expected under the circumstances.

CASSANDRA We need to hold Lady C in our hearts and send her healing thoughts. So sad for her that she missed his funeral.

HONEY I've pushed the boat out for afternoon tea and bought a special treat to cheer us up.

CASSANDRA Don't think I could eat a thing.

HONEY Chocolate biscuit?

WALKER Chocolate? Not our normal plain ones?

HONEY No. These are extra thick chocolate biscuits as it's such a ....

CASSANDRA ...significant day.

HONEY Exactly.

CASSANDRA Thank you Honey I will.

COLONEL Thick biscuits!

WALKER You mean the ones we now get once a year at Christmas with the extra thick chocolate over buttery shortbread.

COLONEL I say.

WALKER *(poshly)* This is not just any biscuit this is a special biscuit.

COLONEL	That's very good Walker. Somebody should turn that into an advert.
WALKER	Thank you Colonel. Am rather proud of that.
HONEY	Here's your biscuit gentlemen.

Honey stuffs their mouths with a biscuit each.

GEORGE	You're all crackers.
IRIS	They're biscuits George. Not crackers. Two words, five and three letters. Lunatic broken earthenware.
GEORGE	Come again Iris?
IRIS	Two words, five and three letters. Lunatic broken earthenware.
GEORGE	Let me have a go at this....
COLONEL	It's easy I can tell you.
GEORGE	Wait a minute.
COLONEL	He's so slow!
GEORGE	Got it!
IRIS	You have?
COLONEL	That's a first.
GEORGE	Crack pot. That's it. Five and three. Crack, pot. You all inspired me. I wouldn't normally get the answer. Iris' clues are impossible.
IRIS	Cryptic not impossible.
GEORGE	Impossible. A conspiracy to make me feel stupid.
WALKER	There's only one man 'ere who's involved in a conspiracy.
GEORGE	What do you mean?

Walker whispers in George's ear but receives no reaction, Sam opens the door as he enters with Cornwallis.

CORNWALLIS	All will be well Sam. Have no fear you will be well looked after.
SAM	Just me?

CORNWALLIS You will all be well looked after. Everything will become clear soon enough *(turning to residents)* Good afternoon everybody. I am just dropping by to express my deep gratitude to you for the support and love you showed Lord Cornwallis this morning. It was very touching to see you all attend with the great and good from all over the county.

IRIS Why wasn't Lady Cornwallis at the funeral?

CASSANDRA Iris, now's not the time.

CORNWALLIS Mama was...indisposed.

IRIS Is she unwell?

CORNWALLIS It was all too much for her. She is, as you would expect...

CASSANDRA Distraught.

CORNWALLIS ...rather...

COLONEL Devastated.

WALKER Deranged with grief.

Pause as everybody looks daggers at Walker and he doesn't understand why.

CORNWALLIS Mama is a touch emotional. But she will pull through this. She's made of stern stuff.

COLONEL Hear hear.

CORNWALLIS It's in the genes.

GEORGE *(cynically)* Huh!

All look at George but nobody cares about his reaction.

CORNWALLIS The Cornwallis name and character lives on in me and I will fight tooth and nail to preserve my dear father's legacy.

SAM Thank you Lord Cornwallis. I think that is something everybody wanted to hear.

CORNWALLIS Of course, of course. You are all an important part of this house.

COLONEL *(low)* We have been for decades.

CORNWALLIS I wish to convey Mama's heartfelt thanks for your support.

(MORE)

CORNWALLIS (cont)
I am pleased to report she is bearing up under the strain of the last few days. What has brought her succour at this dark time is the knowledge that her husband is now at peace after months of pain. She was not up to the funeral I'm afraid. She was desperate to attend but found herself unable to get out of bed and has been confined there for a few days. Thank you once again for your support and kind words. The care of my Mama must now be my number one priority.

Cornwallis turns to leave. Honey stops in shock.

HONEY Lady C is confined to bed?

Honey, carrying tea, and Cornwallis bump together. Tea spills all over his shirt.

CORNWALLIS *(anger)* Look what you have done! You idiot, you f... *(fake concern)* Fine, it's only tea. All down my Hawes and Curtis shirt. Never mind. I must change.

HONEY I'm so sorry Sir. I didn't see you Sir. It was an accident Sir.

CORNWALLIS *(to himself)* Stupid woman.

Cornwallis exits. Honey starts to sob. Sam stands there awkwardly and is torn about following Cornwallis.

CASSANDRA *(hugging Honey)* Don't worry Honey that wasn't your fault.

WALKER I saw it. It were an accident.

IRIS He walked into you dear. Not the other way around.

COLONEL Hear, hear.

HONEY *(tearful)* I spilled tea all down his front. His shirts cost a fortune.

WALKER Cost more than stayin' a week in this place.

COLONEL Is that possible?

All laugh.

HONEY Thanks everybody. You always manage to lighten the mood somehow.

CASSANDRA Aren't you going to say anything Sam?

Sam becomes awkward and embarrassed.

SAM	Why? It was an unfortunate accident. Nobody's fault. Lord Cornwallis was not to blame.
COLONEL	Honey is a member of your staff.
WALKER	Your only staff and you are ....
CASSANDRA	.....close.
SAM	Close, we're not close. That wouldn't be professional.
HONEY	We're not close, we're colleagues, well not colleagues, he's more senior than me. He doesn't like me in that way. We're work mates. Mates, did I say mates, I didn't mean mates, we work together. Yes we just work together.

Honey exits in a hurry. Sam automatically follows her.

WALKER	Sure! Just colleagues.
IRIS	Four letter word beginning L with the clue...

Walker takes a cushion and holds it lustily.

WALKER	Lust, lust, lust! That cleanin' cupboard could tell a tale or two.
IRIS	Walker do you have to? You know LOVE is the answer.
CASSANDRA	Love is the answer to everything. And so is kindness. *(to Walker)* You do know you've upset her?
COLONEL	Sam will look after her.
WALKER	Oh yes Sam'll look after 'er and give 'er....
ALL	Stop!

Lights down.

SCENE SEVEN

Honey is annoyed as she enters the cleaning cupboard and sits down. Sam comes to the door.

SAM	Honey, are you okay? Can I come in?
HONEY	That was so embarrassing.

Sam comes in and sits down.

SAM	I know.
HONEY	They all think something's going on...between us.
SAM	And it isn't.
HONEY	Isn't it?
SAM	No. Absolutely not. That wouldn't be professional.
HONEY	It's so important to be professional.
SAM	Exactly. Is this what's been bothering you?

Honey nods reluctantly.

SAM	There's nothing between us, of course not, you understand.

Honey nods.

SAM	I'm pleased you understand. I don't like you in that way. I can't. We work together. As your manager I must be careful. I can't be seen to...
HONEY	I understand.

Sam places his hand tenderly on Honey

SAM	Good. Don't worry about his shirt. It will all come out in the wash.
HONEY	*(chuckles)* I'll make sure it does. Thanks.

Sam and Honey 'have a moment' staring into each others eyes.

HONEY	Do you think Lady C is okay? I can't imagine her being confined to her bed all day.
SAM	Lord John's death must have affected her badly.
HONEY	Hopefully we can see her soon. *(pause)* He acted so strangely when Iris asked why she wasn't at the funeral.
SAM	Lord Cornwallis?
HONEY	It wasn't natural. He seemed very uncomfortable.
SAM	*(corporate)* Lord Cornwallis is doing his best in very trying circumstances. Iris had a cheek to ask about Lady C in that way.
HONEY	Sorry?

SAM	Lord Cornwallis is not just looking out for his mother. He is looking out for us all.
HONEY	You don't think his reaction was strange?
SAM	Of course not. I blame Iris. She always has to ask a million questions.

Honey stands.

HONEY	I don't believe you. What's got into you? Iris had every right.

Honey is about to exit.

SAM	Don't go.
HONEY	I'm going.
SAM	Not yet.
HONEY	Need to start the supper.
SAM	That can wait. Stay. Just a minute.
HONEY	Is that an order?
SAM	Order? Honey, what is it?
HONEY	Nothing. Let me pass.
SAM	Tell me.
HONEY	Let me pass.
SAM	I can help.
HONEY	No you can't. I'm sure you've got bigger and better things to be doing.
SAM	Honey, don't go. What is it?

Honey pushes past and runs out. Sam follows. Lights down.

SAM	Honey, don't go. Honey, come back. Let's not argue. What did I say?

Lights down.

SCENE EIGHT

Lights up. Forest Lounge. Two weeks later. Morning. Colonel reads the paper, Iris does a crossword, Walker texts, Cassandra is meditating. George enters unseen. Cassandra opens one eye and when she speaks loudly George jumps.

CASSANDRA Something feels off?

WALKER	Wasn't me.
CASSANDRA	I said feels.
WALKER	Oops.
COLONEL	Well it's past coffee time for one thing.
CASSANDRA	Something unsettling is approaching.
GEORGE	*(joking)* It's not me is it?
CASSANDRA	*(serious)* The bad news. It's about to fall.

Cassandra whispers to Iris who nods in understanding.

WALKER	Who's goin' to fall? Only a few weeks since the last funeral.
IRIS	Three letters. Clue, Layoff tool.
COLONEL	*(pondering)* Layoff tool?
IRIS	Yes, three letters.
WALKER	Tool? George *(pause)* Perhaps you'd like to answer?

All hold their breath then laugh.

GEORGE	*(unsure)* Axe?
IRIS	*(surprised)* That's right. You are improving.
CASSANDRA	The axe is about to fall. We're all feeling it.
WALKER	I'm not.
CASSANDRA	Those of us who have feelings.
WALKER	Are you sayin' I 'ave no emotion, I feel no pain, no joy, no sorrow that I am a dry 'usk of a man?
CASSANDRA	No. But you're not in touch with your inner being or your greater divine power.
WALKER	Cor, she thinks I'm divine!
GEORGE	Oh come on Cassandra! You're flying off into the realms of fantasy again.
CASSANDRA	It's not flying off George it's being switched ON. One day you'll learn that and perhaps you'll join me on a wondrous adventure into the vast universe of potential....

Cassandra floats off somewhere.

GEORGE	*(aside)* Nothingness.

IRIS	You underestimate her. If you knew what she achieved in the past, how she helped in the w....
GEORGE	*(aside)* It's a mad house.
COLONEL	10.34. Where's our coffee. It's late!
WALKER	Nice watch Colonel. Don't believe I've had the pleasure of seein' this one before.
COLONEL	Rolex. Doesn't often get an airing.
ALL	Oooo!
WALKER	Looks like a...
COLONEL	1968 Daytona.
WALKER	With a ...
COLONEL	White and red dial.
WALKER	Where d'ya get it?
COLONEL	Birthday present from the family.
ALL	Ooooo!
WALKER	The big red. Same as...
COLONEL	Paul Newman.
ALL	Ooooo....
CASSANDRA	Let's get to the point in hand shall we?
IRIS	Five letters. Cards dealt to crew members.
COLONEL	Hands.

Iris nods. Colonel is overjoyed that he got the answer.

COLONEL	Yes, got one!
WALKER	*(unconvincingly)* Great.

All residents go back to what they had been doing and George looks around the room. Cassandra suddenly does a sharp intake of breath.

IRIS	What is it Cassandra?
CASSANDRA	Honey is on her way.
COLONEL	With our coffee?
CASSANDRA	*(ignoring Colonel)* She's had bad news.
GEORGE	*(sarcastic)* You're not trying to tell us something ridiculous like Honey's got the axe?

CASSANDRA	It's bad news.
IRIS	Are you disrespecting Cassandra and her gift?
GEORGE	I wouldn't dare. But I don't see Honey.

All residents go back to what they'd been doing. Hearing something Colonel puts down his newspaper. Enter Honey and only The Colonel notices her.

COLONEL	Attention! Stand by your beds.

All residents rise in shock and George salutes.

CASSANDRA	*(to George)* Don't worry, you'll get used to it. It's just his way. You don't need to salute.
GEORGE	No. Damn it.
COLONEL	*(to Honey)* About time. Where's our coffee? Honey, it's late. Honey?

Honey stares into space.

IRIS	What's happened?

Silence.

COLONEL	Shell shock. Over to you Woo Woo.
CASSANDRA	Are you okay? Honey?
HONEY	A shock.
CASSANDRA	What?
HONEY	Sad, so sad.
CASSANDRA	Come and sit down. You look like you need a drink.

Cassandra signals to Walker who opens a hidden stash to pull out a small bottle of brandy.

COLONEL	Emergency. None of your half measures.

Walker is shocked to see Colonel open another stash with a large bottle of brandy which he hands to Cassandra to pour. As soon as she has finished pouring Walker takes the bottle and cradles it like a baby. Honey drinks and the brandy is strong.

HONEY	Wow!
COLONEL	Bull's eye. That hit the mark.

Honey doesn't like the brandy and hands it back much to the dismay of Walker.

HONEY	I've been hit *(pointing to chest)* right here.
IRIS	What's happened?
CASSANDRA	Honey are you okay?

Honey nods.

HONEY	Bad news.
WALKER	Bad news.
HONEY	*(vaguely)* Yes.
WALKER	Millennium Bug finally bitten?
IRIS	Walker, be quiet!
HONEY	I've been dismissed.
COLONEL	No!
IRIS	What do you mean dismissed?
HONEY	Lord Christopher Cornwallis has made me redundant.
COLONEL	Redundant? Cornwallis can't do that!
CASSANDRA	How awful!
IRIS	Why would he do that?
GEORGE	It's Cornwallis, you're not surprised are you?
HONEY	Have to leave in two weeks.

Honey stands in a daze centre stage in a noisy farcical scene where all residents try to push one another out of the way in an attempt to comfort Honey.

HONEY	Cornwallis is a monster.
WALKER	*(to residents)* Did you hear that? 'Oney called Cornwallis a monster. 'Oney said monster.
COLONEL	*(to residents)* The worm is turning.
CASSANDRA	He is a monster Honey.
GEORGE	There must be something we can do.
HONEY	There's nothing we can do.
COLONEL	That can't be true.
IRIS	We can't do without you Honey.
WALKER	There 'aint no way you're goin'.

GEORGE	Cornwallis strikes again.
CASSANDRA	Let me give you a healing hug.
WALKER	What are we goin' to do without you? Who's goin' to make our meals?
COLONEL	*(pointing at his watch)* And our coffee?
CASSANDRA	Colonel, can you stop thinking about your stomach for one moment.
COLONEL	But it's a large part of my life.
CASSANDRA	We know.
HONEY	To cut costs all your meals will be delivered by van.

General uproar.

CASSANDRA	A van! That's awful.
WALKER	No way!
COLONEL	Eating out of a van. Insupportable. I can't have this.
HONEY	I don't want to leave. I want to carry on cooking for you. I love this place and this job with you.
CASSANDRA	We love you too!
IRIS	You're so special to us.
WALKER	You're the best.
COLONEL	Here, here.
GEORGE	I've not been here long but you seem pretty decent to me.
HONEY	Thank you George and you seem pretty decent to me.
GEORGE	Thank you.
IRIS	Where's Sam?

All stop to hear the reply.

HONEY	With Cornwallis. I don't understand what's going on.
IRIS	Is he redundant?
WALKER	'E's always been a drip but I wouldn't 'ave called him that.

IRIS   Has Sam been made redundant?

Honey shakes her head.

GEORGE   So the cost cutting exercise doesn't include the closing of the home. *(aside)* At this stage.

IRIS   Who said anything about the home closing?

WALKER   What do you know George?

COLONEL   Tell us.

GEORGE   Why would I know anything?

WALKER   You know more than you're lettin' on.

GEORGE   There is one thing.

COLONEL   Tell us.

GEORGE   I don't trust Cornwallis.

WALKER   If Cornwallis is up to somethin' I could call my contact at ....

IRIS   Don't tell me I don't want to know.

WALKER   ...and I could lean on him. 'Ard.

IRIS   Poor chap.

WALKER   Don't feel sorry for 'im, 'e's conducted Olympic leanin' for many years. Bout time 'e tasted some of 'is own medicine.

IRIS   A very bitter medicine.

WALKER   Of course. So I can gently remind... Mr. X that 'e owes me after all the favours I did for 'im durin that Willow Grove deal few years back when...

IRIS   Don't tell me I don't want to know.

WALKER   Yes, better you don't know.

GEORGE   And you shouldn't trust Cornwallis either.

IRIS   Are you trying to push the focus onto Cornwallis?

GEORGE   What do you mean?

Walker pins George into a corner.

WALKER   Focus on Cornwallis so we don't point the finger of suspicion at you.

(MORE)

WALKER (cont)
What do you know about Newfield Housin'?
Why are you speakin' to Newfield Housin'? 'As
Newfield Housin' got anythin' to do with the
future of the manor.

GEORGE   What are you talking about?

WALKER   I think you know. I don't trust you.

GEORGE   It's Cornwallis you shouldn't trust.

WALKER   I'm not so sure.

Sam enters and the room goes quiet.

COLONEL   Honey's been made redundant. And you?

Sam pulls out a piece of paper which he reads with no emotion.

SAM   Lord Cornwallis has asked me to read this.
'Dear Residents. I thank you for your patience.
Certain unnecessary overheads must be
trimmed in a cost cutting exercise aimed at
making Beeches Manor Residential Home run
more efficiently and effectively with a trickle-
down positive effect on residents. Thank you
once again for your forbearance.' That is all.

Silence. Honey, who Sam has not noticed, appears behind him.

HONEY   So I must be *(mimics Cornwallis)* the
unnecessary overhead that must be trimmed in a
cost cutting exercise with a trickle-down
positive effect on residents.

SAM   No Honey. No.

Honey exits in tears.

WALKER   *(to Sam)* So?

SAM   So, what?

WALKER   Are you goin' to run after Honey? You can
comfort her again. Or are you staying 'ere.

GEORGE   And tell us what's going on?

WALKER   Tell us!

*Sam will not say anything more. Sam should stay to calm the
residents but runs after Honey. All residents are in shock.*

GEORGE   *(aside)* I need to make a call.

George exits.

WALKER	Where's he goin'?
COLONEL	Highly suspicious. Again.
IRIS	Stop! Before this descends into further chaos... We need to work this all out. Everybody go back to your rooms. Call anybody you know - particularly you with your housing contacts Walker - contact everybody and let's find out what is happening.
WALKER	Will do.
COLONEL	Good plan Iris. No time to waste. Chop, chop everybody.

All exit. Lights down.

SCENE NINE

Lights up. Same morning. Small dark room in the manor house. Lady Cornwallis sits in her chair leaning forward onto the table. Enter Cornwallis with some pills and paperwork.

CORNWALLIS Hello Mother. Time for your pills.

LADY C Again?

CORNWALLIS Time flies doesn't it. Here take these.

Lady C has very little energy and Cornwallis has to hold the glass while she sips and she has difficulty swallowing the pills.

CORNWALLIS You're in a bit of state this morning aren't you? Never mind. I won't take up too much of your time. I just need you to help with some of the boring bureaucracy that's arisen following the funeral. Please sign here.

LADY C I can't.

CORNWALLIS Yes you can Mother. I'll help you hold the pen.

LADY C I would like to read the papers first.

CORNWALLIS You don't need to do that. It's only boring stuff to do with payments after the funeral.

LADY C I need more time. I feel so tired since John died it must be the shock.

CORNWALLIS Of course Mother. I'll leave the papers here.

Cornwallis puts the papers onto the table.

CORNWALLIS I'm concerned about the house Mother. The builders have found more problems with the ceilings.

LADY C The roof was repaired only a few years ago thanks to Cecil.

CORNWALLIS The roof but not the ceilings Mother. They are all falling down and it will cost a fortune to fix. That's why it is so cold here. Wouldn't you prefer to be in a modern heated house?

LADY C I like it here.

CORNWALLIS So do I mother. There are so many memories but we'll always have those no matter where we are. Remember when I was little and we'd play hide and seek. I don't know how you did it, even in this big house you always found me.

LADY C I know you well son. I know your likes and dislikes.

CORNWALLIS I'd like you to sign. Please.

LADY C I want to live out my days here.

CORNWALLIS Fine, no pressure I'm only thinking of what's best for you. Since I've looked at the paperwork father left I've come to realise just how much needs to be done to the house. I want to keep you safe and warm.

LADY C Thank you for your concern but I will only leave Beeches Manor in a wooden box.

CORNWALLIS Please don't talk like that Mother. I can't bear it.

LADY C It comes to us all Christopher.

CORNWALLIS Yes. *(softly)* I must go.

Cornwallis picks up the papers unseen by Lady C and exits. Lights down.

SCENE TEN

Lights up. Cleaning cupboard. Same morning.

SAM Sorry Honey. You know this has nothing to do with me. It's the last thing I'd want.

HONEY And yet I'm still redundant.

SAM	It's out of my hands.
HONEY	What am I going to do?
SAM	I'll help you find a new job.
HONEY	You. Help me?
SAM	Of course.
HONEY	Why would you do that?
SAM	Because....Just because. I will do my very best.
HONEY	I don't need your help thanks.
SAM	You don't want my help?
HONEY	No.
SAM	Why?
HONEY	Just because.

Awkward pause. Honey softens.

HONEY	What's going on Sam?
SAM	*(corporate)* Lord Cornwallis was shocked to discover that the residential home's overheads are greater than previously stated and he's been forced to institute cost cutting measures.
HONEY	That's what he said. What do you think's going on?
SAM	Exactly that.
HONEY	But as Home Manager it would have been your job to work out the overheads.
SAM	I must have made errors in my calculations.
HONEY	Are you sure?
SAM	I believe that is the case.
HONEY	Will you be made redundant?
SAM	I have a duty to care for the residents and their well being.
HONEY	And the home will continue?
SAM	I will continue to care for the residents.
HONEY	That's it. I've tried to talk to you like a human being but all I get is a cold, corporate robot.

SAM	That's not true.
HONEY	Then speak to me from the heart.
CORNWALLIS	*(offstage)* Sam! Sam! Where are you?
SAM	Got to go. Let's talk more later. I want to help.
HONEY	I give up.

Lights down.

SCENE ELEVEN

Lights up. Forest Lounge. Two weeks later 7.20pm. Cornwallis enters carrying a laptop case.

CORNWALLIS Harris! Potter! You're needed in the Forest Lounge.

Cornwallis goes to take down his father's portrait. Sam rushes in and Cornwallis pretends to be straightening the portrait.

CORNWALLIS That was quicker than... Ready for the meeting?

SAM Um.

CORNWALLIS Good. It's very straightforward. We have no choice blah, blah, blah...We've spent past month after my father's funeral trying to make things work blah, blah, blah...financial pressures blah, blah, blah. Got that?

SAM I'm to tell them?

CORNWALLIS As Manager of Beeches Manor Residential Home this news is your responsibility. I'm doing you a favour by being here.

SAM As it's to do with the house I think it would be better coming from you.

CORNWALLIS The Manager is personally liable for all residents and their well being.

SAM Personally liable?

CORNWALLIS Naturally. As Manager you are responsible for the running of the home so you hold all the risk. The owner is dependent on and vulnerable to your actions with regard to the residents.

SAM Even though I don't have any authority and must do exactly as you say?

CORNWALLIS	Have you read the revised employment contract?
SAM	I haven't had a chance. Since your father died I've been too busy organising everything and everybody. *(assertively)* I think they would appreciate this news coming from you.
CORNWALLIS	No.
SAM	I just can't do it.
CORNWALLIS	It's your job.
SAM	I can't.
CORNWALLIS	That is not my problem.
SAM	But Sir.

Awkward pause. Residents, except George, enter slowly. Cornwallis and Sam are in their own worlds.

WALKER	Not late are we Colonel?
COLONEL	*(showing his watch)* Seven twenty nine. We're one minute early old chap.
WALKER	What is it this time? Do you know Cassandra?
CASSANDRA	I foresee more bad news.
COLONEL	Is this about food in a van? I'll have his guts for...

Colonel heads angrily towards Cornwallis but is steered away by Iris just as Cornwallis becomes aware of the residents.

IRIS	*(breezily)* Did you enjoy your supper Colonel?
COLONEL	Rather. Love Honey's meals. At least they are not from a ...
IRIS	Thank you Colonel. Let's all sit down.

Iris helps Colonel to sit down. He doesn't make this easy as he wants to get back to Cornwallis and both end up laughing.

CORNWALLIS	Very disappointing Sam. Clearly you're not up to this. I'm taking over. Stand aside.
SAM	Thank you.
CORNWALLIS	This will be quick and efficient.
SAM	*(sarcastic)* Yes Sir, of course Sir.
CORNWALLIS	No room for sentiment.

SAM	Of course not Sir.
CORNWALLIS	Lance the boil.
SAM	Yes Sir.
CORNWALLIS	For the best.
SAM	I'm sure.
IRIS	Sit!

Enter George who notices Colonel and Iris laughing.

GEORGE	Everybody is bright and breezy this evening.
COLONEL	Any reason we shouldn't be?
GEORGE	We'll soon see.

Cornwallis turns to speak to the residents.

CORNWALLIS	Good evening residents.
ALL	*(mumbles and groans)* Evening.
CORNWALLIS	Thank you for gathering here.
COLONEL	At coffee time. Where is coffee?
CORNWALLIS	Thank you Colonel, I'm sure Honey's on her way. Sam can you check please.

Sam turns just as Honey enters and they nearly collide.

SAM	Here she is Sir.
WALKER	*(lasciviously to Sam)* See, you are close.
HONEY	Here I am. My last but one evening coffee run.
COLONEL	Damn it!
CORNWALLIS	*(carries on regardless)* Thank you for gathering here this evening.
WALKER	Bet Cornwallis won't be eatin' from no van.
IRIS	No frozen meals for the Lord.
CASSANDRA	No processed food full of E numbers and additives for him.

George who has been sitting quietly stands.

GEORGE	It might be worth hearing what he has to say. Could you at least try and keep quiet?

Everybody is stunned.

CORNWALLIS *(to Sam)* Who's this?

SAM   George. He took Cecil's room.

ALL   *(cross themselves)* Cecil.

COLONEL   May he rest in peace.

WALKER   And enjoy the miseries of the afterlife.

CASSANDRA   The afterlife won't be miserable...

WALKER   Then Cecil won't be 'appy.

CASSANDRA   Fair point.

COLONEL   We miss you Cecil.

All stare at George who gives up and sits down again.

COLONEL   We really miss you.

CASSANDRA   Four weeks to the day before The Boss.

One by one Colonel, Walker, Cassandra and Iris stand, place one arm across their chest, bow their heads to the portrait.

IRIS   To The Boss.

COL/W/CAS   The Boss.

COLONEL   May he rest in peace.

CASSANDRA   A kind man.

IRIS   The best of men.

WALKER   The real deal.

CORNWALLIS This has nothing to do with my father.

George stands.

GEORGE   Why won't you listen!

COLONEL   What do you mean? We are listening.

CASSANDRA   Of course we are.

WALKER   I'm all ears.

CORNWALLIS Thanks for trying George. This is impossible.

IRIS   Six letter word. Clue 'Attempting to hear'

Nobody answers

SAM   *(softly)* Trying.

IRIS   Correct. Very trying.

CORNWALLIS *(to Sam)* I am only going to say this once.

SAM Everybody please be quiet. Lord Cornwallis has something important to say. *(to himself)* And I don't want to be the one to tell you.

CORNWALLIS I have a very important announcement. *(putting on a glum face)* With regret I need to inform you that I must sell Beeches Manor and therefore this residential home will close in the near future.

Sharp intake of breath. Lights down.

ACT TWO

SCENE ONE

Lights up. Forest Lounge following on from Act One.

CORNWALLIS With regret I need to inform you that I must sell Beeches Manor and therefore this residential home will close in the near future.

Silence. All residents are in shock except George who isn't at all surprised but hides himself from Cornwallis' gaze.

CORNWALLIS If there had been any other option we would have taken it. There was really no other way.

Silence.

SAM They're in shock.

HONEY How could he do this? *(to Sam)* How could you?

SAM This wasn't my decision.

HONEY *(to Cornwallis)* The residents have lived here for years. To move them now will be extremely harmful. You can't do this. You can't.

As Cornwallis talks Colonel sneaks up behind him SAS style.

CORNWALLIS My hands are tied. My father's death has revealed incredible debts secured against the manor due, I hate to admit this, due to my father's fondness for a bet. It has become clear that it is no longer sustainable to continue the home and regrettably we are left with no other choice than to sell. You will need to find new accommodation within four weeks.

IRIS *(to residents)* Lord John Cornwallis was no gambler. *(to Cornwallis)* Let me get this straight.

Colonel is about to administer one of his secret death chops.

COLONEL *(to residents)* I'll make him straight.

CASSANDRA Keep calm Colonel.

Colonel is stopped by Cassandra who sweeps her arms over his head and he goes faint, falling into her arms. Cornwallis turns.

CORNWALLIS What's going on?

Cassandra has to pretend she has been hugging Colonel lovingly as he stirs and wants to hit Cornwallis.

CASSANDRA   Pardon us Lord Cornwallis.

When Cornwallis turns away Cassandra and Colonel tidy themselves in disgust. Cassandra leads Colonel to his chair.

IRIS   *(rational and calm)* You're saying your father gambled away your inheritance and now you must sell Beeches Manor to cover his debts meaning we must move out within four weeks.

CORNWALLIS Correct.

Walker sidles up to Cornwallis.

WALKER   My Lord, who's the deal with then. Whose buyin' this 'ouse?

CORNWALLIS A once in a lifetime offer has been made for the manor by a prestigious organisation.

WALKER   Called...?

CORNWALLIS Private.

CASSANDRA   Where are we meant to go?

COLONEL   You can't expect us to leave. We belong here.

IRIS   Surely there are other things you can do to repay any debts?

CORNWALLIS Sam. Take over. The Home Manager must address questions regarding future accommodation. I must leave.

SAM   Um, yes, yes of course.

Colonel renews his efforts to get to Cornwallis but is prevented by Cassandra who sweeps her arms over his head and he calms down and collapses into his chair.

WALKER   *(sidling up to Cornwallis)* The amount we pay to stay here, this business must be a real money spinner eh? Are there any capital assets you could push in my direction? I know a man who might be interested in...

CORNWALLIS *(ignoring Walker)* Wrap it up Sam.

Silence. Cornwallis turns to go.

IRIS   Before you go Lord Christopher Cornwallis of The Cornwallis family owners of The Beeches Manor estate, Little Cracknell...

CORNWALLIS   What?

IRIS   Son of Lord John Cornwallis...

COLONEL   Lord John Cornwallis!

The Colonel in his chair salutes and they all bow their heads.

CORNWALLIS   What of it?

IRIS   Whose family has owned this grand house for over two hundred years...

CORNWALLIS   Get on with it woman!

IRIS   Generations of the Cornwallis family brought up and lived out their lives within these very walls....

CORNWALLIS   Spit it out.

IRIS   Why?

CORNWALLIS   Why?

IRIS   Why are you selling up?

CORNWALLIS   I have told you why.

IRIS   We need to know.

CORNWALLIS   No you don't.

IRIS   Where will your mother live? She loves the manor.

CORNWALLIS   How dare you! I refuse to answer to all of you. You know everything you need to know. Beeches Manor is being sold and you have to leave. Full stop.

IRIS   Well this is a *(stressing the words)* Funny Business.

All residents, except George, look at each other and nod. Iris whispers orders to Walker, Cassandra and Colonel.

IRIS   Get me his laptop!

CASSANDRA   *(to Cornwallis)* Let me at least clear your energy to give you luck with the sale of the estate.

Cassandra begins sweeping arm movements around Cornwallis to clear his energy. He is uncomfortable and irritated.

CORNWALLIS Get off woman!

COLONEL Don't do that Cassandra. Stop it.

WALKER What is it Colonel?

COLONEL It reminds me of The Falklands. The blades of the helicopters as they swooped into Goose Green.

Colonel goes into a trance state and deliberately bumps into Cornwallis who goes flying onto a chair and Walker deftly opens the case, takes out the laptop and replaces it with a large empty bottle. Walker hands laptop to Iris who immediately opens the laptop and secretly begins to try to crack Cornwallis' password.

IRIS *(aside)* If you won't tell us then I'll find out myself.

COLONEL Cease, desist, stand down. Take cover everybody.

Colonel pushes Cornwallis onto a chair and jumps onto him as he flails trying to get up.

COLONEL Keep down, keep down. Overhead attack.

Sam tries to help but is distracted by Cassandra. Walker signals mission complete to Cassandra.

CASSANDRA Colonel, you're having one of your turns *(insincerely to Cornwallis)* Sir, let me help you up. Oh dear, can't, my back, ouch, chiropractor said I mustn't strain it.

Everybody is too busy to help Cornwallis get up which he eventually does. George has looked on bemused.

GEORGE What are you all doing?

CORNWALLIS I have never been so insulted. You all deserve what's coming. Sam, Sam!

SAM Yes Sir.

CORNWALLIS Take over. *(to residents)* You're ridiculous. You're all ridiculous.

HONEY They didn't mean to!

The Colonel stands in front of Cornwallis.

CORNWALLIS Move aside!

COLONEL Beg your pardon?

CORNWALLIS Out of my way.

COLONEL Sorry can't hear you. Bit deaf.

HONEY *(to Sam)* Take him away. Quickly!

Sam leads Cornwallis out of The Colonel's path.

SAM This way sir.

CORNWALLIS I wash my hands of this lot. Sam, you are personally liable. You sort them out.

Cornwallis exits. Sam is left confused.

COLONEL Personally liable! You're in his pocket Sam.

WALKER 'E's stitched you right up.

SAM I have a duty of care to all residents which I will carry out to the best of my abilities.

Sam exits. Honey collects the cups and leaves.

SCENE TWO

COLONEL Good riddance.

Iris works hard on the laptop.

IRIS There's no way The Boss was a gambler. I'm going to prove that very quickly.

GEORGE What on earth was that about?

CASSANDRA Iris gave us the signal.

GEORGE What signal?

COLONEL THE signal.

GEORGE None the wiser. Iris? What's that?

COLONEL Nothing to do with you.

GEORGE That's Cornwallis' laptop!

WALKER No, it's not it's mine.

COLONEL It just looks the same.

WALKER Iris is fixin' it for me.

GEORGE	Yeah, right. Let's stop all the nonsense and use his laptop to catch Cornwallis out.
IRIS	*(head deep in the laptop)* Two steps ahead of you.
WALKER	What's the deal with you and Cornwallis?
GEORGE	He's not to be trusted.
WALKER	Why d'ya think that?
GEORGE	No reason... I'm a scientist.
WALKER	So?
GEORGE	Scientists evaluate the available data. If it looks like a duck, waddles like a duck and quacks like a duck it is....
COLONEL	He's not a duck. Ducks are too likeable. Christopher Cornwallis is a, a, a .....
IRIS	One more minute... A four letter amphibian with dry warty skin?
GEORGE	One of your crossword clues?

Iris nods.

GEORGE	Frog? Newt? Lizard? Can't think.

Iris shakes her head in shame. George doesn't catch on for a considerable time.

COLONEL	He's a toad. A cold reptile who cares nothing for us. If I get my hands on him he'll be toad smoothie.
CASSANDRA	Watch your blood pressure Colonel. Let's give Iris some space to crack his password.
IRIS	It's done.
ALL	Already!
GEORGE	No way, not that quickly, that's not possible.
IRIS	It is.
WALKER	She was the best in 'er secret organisation... you know...sounds like a furniture shop.
GEORGE	Ikea?
WALKER	No. MFI.
GEORGE	Where?

WALKER	She's the real deal.
CASSANDRA	Creme de la creme.
IRIS	Still the best.
COLONEL	I second that.
WALKER	Third it.

Cassandra waves her arms around to 'move the energy'

CASSANDRA	The fourth is with you.
GEORGE	What is going on?
COLONEL	Time is ticking. What have we got Iris?

Iris holds up a memory stick.

IRIS	Everything we need is on this.
WALKER	What the 'eck?
IRIS	A portable memory bank.
WALKER	Data from the computer goes on this?
IRIS	Of course. Technology is developing rapidly.
WALKER	But I've never seen anythin' this small before, nothin' this powerful. How d'ya get this?
IRIS	I could tell you but I'd have to shoot you.
COLONEL	She's not joking.
CASSANDRA	Cool. But not as cool as the human brain.
IRIS	Just more reliable.
CASSANDRA	You're probably right.
IRIS	I've downloaded all relevant files from the laptop onto here so we don't need this anymore.
GEORGE	Wow!

Iris carefully places the laptop on a table.

CASSANDRA	That's awesome.
IRIS	No time for gawping. Colonel what is the time?
COLONEL	Seven forty nine General.
GEORGE	General?
COLONEL	Just a nickname.

IRIS	We need to work this all through. There are still pieces of this enigma we need to uncover.
COLONEL	*(laughs)* Enigma. Good one Iris.

All laugh apart from George.

GEORGE	Why's that funny?
IRIS	Work it out George. It's code for my former life.

All laugh apart from George.

IRIS	Give me an hour to work on this in my room. Beech Nuts session here at twenty one hundred hours. All agreed.
ALL	Agreed.
GEORGE	Beech Nut session?
COLONEL	You'll find out at twenty one hundred hours.

All exit except George who addresses Lord John's portrait.

GEORGE	Please tell me, what is going on? You held them in such high esteem but look at them now. They haven't a clue. I need to sort this out by myself.

George takes out his mobile to make a call.

GEORGE	James any info from Newfield yet? Nothing substantive then? Anything on Cornwallis? His lawyers said what? *(in shock)* Lady Cornwallis? No! Are you sure? Congratulations James. That's a game changer. How much did it cost me to get that nugget? Worth every penny. You will get a bonus too. My pleasure. Got to go. Thanks.

George rushes out. Lights down.

SCENE THREE

Lights up. Cleaning cupboard. That evening. Sam sits on his own looking at his employment contract.

SAM	Has he stitched me up? Has he? No. He's an honourable man. He's been good to me. What if he has stitched me up?

Enter Honey

HONEY	Oh, you're here. Not with your new best friend?
SAM	Don't be like that.
HONEY	Well it's my last day tomorrow so I'm free to say what I like.
SAM	Say it then.
HONEY	I don't believe you!
SAM	What?
HONEY	You with Cornwallis. Yes Sir, no Sir, how else can I serve you Sir?
SAM	I'm doing my job.
HONEY	Are you? Haven't you worked out that he is not Lord John.

Sam shakes his head in despair.

SAM	What am I going to do? How do I help them? There's nowhere for them to go. A month is so little time.
HONEY	Unbelievable.
SAM	I know. This is so hard. You'll help me won't you Honey? I can count on your support?
HONEY	No.

Sam is tongue tied and then blurts out.

SAM	You can't mean that?
HONEY	I do.

Sam reaches out to touch Honey and she moves quickly away.

SAM	What's wrong? I'm saying I need you... your help.
HONEY	No you don't.
SAM	Of course I do.
HONEY	I'm not helping you do harm to others. You need to stand up for what's right.
SAM	I'm trying to....
HONEY	A robot who always does as he's told by that block of ice. Who never stands up to him, even as he destroys others' lives.

SAM	He's my boss. This is my job.
HONEY	It's your job, not your life. Soon I'm sure you won't have this job.
SAM	You think he's going to sack me too?
HONEY	Open your eyes Sam. Look what he's done to me, to the residents, to his father's memory and what has he done to Lady C?
SAM	What are you saying?
HONEY	Cornwallis hasn't let me take food to Lady C for the past month. I'm worried about her. Aren't you?
SAM	No. Well. I hadn't thought about it. Lord Cornwallis is a good man. You don't know him as well as I do. He just needs careful handling.
HONEY	Careful handling? Looks more like total submission.
SAM	You know I've got to keep him onside. He's got great contacts. He'll help me in the future.
HONEY	Do you really believe that?
SAM	Yes. He's very well connected.
HONEY	But only for himself not for others.
SAM	That's not true. He's a real gent.
HONEY	Total submission.
SAM	That's not true.
HONEY	Then it's just about your career.
SAM	No! I'm trying to do the best for everybody. For the residents, the business, for you and me.
HONEY	You and me?
SAM	As the workforce, I mean. Don't you trust me Honey?
HONEY	Before I can trust you, you need to make a decision.
SAM	What?
HONEY	Are you with us or with Cornwallis?

Honey stands

SAM	I can't decide that.
HONEY	You just don't care do you? You're too scared of him. Too scared to do anything.
SAM	I am not scared.
HONEY	You are. I'll admit that I am. He's a horrid, frightening man.
SAM	Is that why you haven't said anything?
HONEY	You think he'd listen to me? He doesn't know I exist other than to clean up. Which is nothing to him. I'm something on the bottom of his shoe.
SAM	You're much more than that.
HONEY	You're the manager and he will listen to you.
SAM	And you're important. Know that.
HONEY	Me important!
SAM	You are. You're important to....

Sam takes Honey's hand.

HONEY	What are you doing?

Sam drops Honey's hand.

SAM	I'm ...Trust me Honey.
HONEY	Trust you?
SAM	Yes.
HONEY	I used to. But I can't say I do right now.
SAM	Why? We've been through so much over the years.
HONEY	And you've always done the right thing as "Manager of The Beeches Manor Residential Home".
SAM	I've tried. Yes.
HONEY	Then stand up for the residents and for yourself for once.
SAM	Honey, Honey.
HONEY	Goodbye Sam.

Honey exits. Lights down.

SCENE FOUR

Lights up. Forest Lounge. A few minutes later. Sam enters.

SAM   *(to Lord John's portrait)* Have I got him all wrong? I know he isn't continuing your legacy but then he has no choice. Under the circumstances, forgive me, he's got to sell. Hasn't he? He had to cut Honey's job? The residents will be okay won't they? Lady Cornwallis is well isn't she? And this amazing opportunity he's found for me in London I can't refuse that. He wouldn't do that if he was stitching me up would he?

Sam collapses into a chair. Enter Cornwallis angrily holding the empty bottle and looking for his laptop. He doesn't see Sam.

CORNWALLIS   What a shower! Good riddance to them! Here you are. They'll pay for messing with my stuff.

Cornwallis throws away the bottle and picks up the laptop. Just as he is about to leave, he notices his father's portrait.

CORNWALLIS   *(disdainful)* This is your mess. I told you inviting them in was ridiculous. You don't need to worry I'll soon have them and this dump of a house sorted for good. Just you see. There's nothing you can do about it now.

Cornwallis laughs, takes down the portrait and tosses it aside. His mobile rings and he takes it out.

CORNWALLIS   George. Great to hear from you. Pleased to say everything is going to plan my end and it will be all wrapped up within the month. *(laughs at caller's reply)* Indeed, Christmas has come very early this year. You still okay to meet for lunch tomorrow at Le Filet? Good, good. Look forward to seeing you and the 72 ounce. Au revoir George.

Cornwallis clears the call.

CORNWALLIS   Bye bye Beeches. I won't be sad to say goodbye to you or this tatty place full of idiots.

Cornwallis kicks the portrait to hide it and exits. Sam runs to the portrait and tenderly picks it up, talks to it and replaces it.

SAM   Thank you for the answer I needed.

Sam bows his head to the portrait and exits. Lights down.

SCENE FIVE

Lights up. Small dark room in the manor house. Lady Cornwallis is asleep in her chair and tosses and turns.

CORNWALLIS Wake up mother.

LADY C No. You can't. Please no.

CORNWALLIS Mother, you're having a bad dream. Wake up.

Cornwallis gently rocks Lady C and she wakes with a jolt.

LADY C Don't do it!

CORNWALLIS It's alright mother. You were having a bad dream that's all.

LADY C A dream?

CORNWALLIS Yes.

LADY C So everything is fine? No gambling debts?

CORNWALLIS It pains me to say the debts are all too real.

LADY C I don't believe it. John wouldn't. You know how careful he had to be with every penny for the sake of the estate. He wouldn't let us all down like that.

CORNWALLIS Believe it mother. It's the sad truth. You must sign these papers now or we will be in big trouble.

LADY C I'm too tired.

CORNWALLIS Please mother. It has to be now.

LADY C Take them away.

Cornwallis turns on the tears.

CORNWALLIS Mother, please. This is the only way.

Silence.

CORNWALLIS I wish father were here. I'm not used to the responsibility of all this. Father took care of everything. I miss him so much. It's all too much. This would help. Please help.

Silence.

CORNWALLIS Mother. You're the only one who can help me. Please!

Silence. Cornwallis bangs the paperwork down onto Lady C's table in anger.

CORNWALLIS Now! *(calms down)* Sorry Mother. I don't want it to be like this but there is no choice. I have no choice. If you don't sign there will be terrible consequences.

LADY C What do you mean?

CORNWALLIS Terrible, ghastly consequences.

LADY C For you?

Cornwallis nods.

LADY C *(gently)* Tell me.

CORNWALLIS They'll come from London and hurt me. They've been known to kill.

LADY C Who?

CORNWALLIS Nasty people.

LADY C *(calmly)* Do you owe a great deal?

CORNWALLIS Enough. Please Mother, help me. Sign this.

LADY C Sorry Christopher. I can't betray your father. We can't sell the Beeches. We must find another way.

Before Cornwallis has a chance to respond the door rattles. Cornwallis can see who it is but not the audience.

CORNWALLIS Who's there? How dare you. Get out of my house.

Lights down.

SCENE SIX

Lights up. Forest Lounge. 9pm. Enter all residents except George.

IRIS Where's George?

COLONEL He wouldn't be any help. Takes him too long to catch on.

IRIS Let's start. *(knocking a table)* I call this session to order.

CASSANDRA	Bless this Beech Nuts session and may it bear the desired fruit.
WALKER	What 'ave you uncovered Iris?
IRIS	The key to unlocking this mystery, the secret code if you will, is the question 'why'. Why does Cornwallis want to sell? If we discover that then we can counter this attack.
COLONEL	Time's ticking Iris.
IRIS	I think Sam and Honey need to hear this.

Walker goes to the door and whistles loudly as if to a dog.

CASSANDRA	Sam won't want to hear this?
IRIS	Maybe not but we can't hide it from him. Surely he'd rather know.

Sam and Honey come rushing into the lounge.

SAM	What's the emergency?
HONEY	Is anybody hurt?
COLONEL	Iris has news.
IRIS	Sam, this might be painful for you. I've discovered the true nature of your highly respected leader.
SAM	He's not respected by me.
HONEY	What? Really?
SAM	Can't stand the man.
HONEY	You do care!

Honey gives Sam a hug which lasts a long time.

SAM	I always have.
HONEY	Welcome back to the real world.
WALKER	Ooo! What's happening 'ere?

Sam and Honey part in embarrassment.

COLONEL	Calm down Walker.

Iris claps her hands.

IRIS	We need to concentrate.
WALKER	Sorry Iris.

SAM	*(embarrassed)* Let's get on.
IRIS	Cornwallis is selling the manor to Newfield Housing. He has a contact there called George Thompson.
WALKER	So that's his real name. It isn't George Lowe.
COLONEL	Where is the traitor? I'll tear him in half.
WALKER	I knew it!
IRIS	I've found extensive correspondence between Cornwallis and this George Thompson. Newfield are offering tens of millions of pounds for the manor and part of the estate and plan to build five hundred new houses. Beeches Manor is only worth £1 million as a residential home.
WALKER	Five 'undred 'ouses. That'll net Newfield a fortune.
CASSANDRA	Why only buy part of the estate?
IRIS	The agreement is that Cornwallis will keep ten acres of land on which to build his brand new designer glass palace.
COLONEL	I'll tear him limb from limb.

All other residents shake their heads.

COLONEL	At least allow me to hurt him badly.

All other residents shake their heads.

CASSANDRA	Colonel really, you can't do that.
COLONEL	I can do it so nobody would ever know.
WALKER	Like the secret death chops you learnt in the war Colonel?
COLONEL	From the Japanese.
WALKER	Wow, show me.
COLONEL	Absolutely not.
WALKER	Go on Colonel.
COLONEL	No.
WALKER	Please. I'd love to know how to do that.
COLONEL	It's not for Joe Public.
WALKER	I'm not Joe Public.

COLONEL	No you're more dangerous.
CASSANDRA	Violence solves nothing Colonel. How many times? You'll be the one who ends up suffering not him. You could end up in jail.
COLONEL	It'd be worth it.
CASSANDRA	Cornwallis is not worth your freedom Colonel.

This stops Colonel in his tracks.

COLONEL	You're right. As ever dear Woo Woo.
IRIS	Have you all totally forgotten the objective of this Beech Nut session. We must find out how to stop this sale.
WALKER	What else did you get from the files?
IRIS	I just need to bypass a few more security barriers. Give me half an hour more. Put your minds to something productive in that time.

Iris taps away on her laptop. Cassandra immediately sits to meditate. Colonel and Walker look lost and wander round the room. Sam grabs Honey by the hand and leads her out of the lounge. Walker whispers to Colonel in a corner.

WALKER	Torture. In Japan didn't they pull out their prisoners' finger nails one by one.
COLONEL	That's just for starters. They'd dig a large hole, stand pointed bamboo poles in it and throw them in.
WALKER	Ouch!
COLONEL	Shhh! Then there's the water torture, that was always very popular...

Cassandra opens one eye.

CASSANDRA	Walker I thought better of you. This negative energy must stop. Don't encourage him. Both of you come here and meditate with me.
COLONEL	Us?
CASSANDRA	Yes you.
WALKER	Now?
CASSANDRA	Well do you have anything better to do?
WALKER	S'pose not.

COLONEL	Can I sit in my chair. My knees aren't what they used to be.
CASSANDRA	Yes. Now be quiet and follow me.

Walker and Colonel obey and copy Cassandra.

CASSANDRA	Just breathe. That's right. And again...

Loud breathing from Walker and Colonel. Lights down.

SCENE SEVEN

Lights up. Cleaning cupboard. Following. Sam pulls Honey into the cleaning cupboard. Sam goes to speak but the words won't come out of his mouth.

HONEY	You do care.

Sam nods.

HONEY	You just weren't able to say.

Sam shakes his head.

HONEY	But you do care.

Sam nods.

SAM	A great deal. About the residents and about....
HONEY	Why didn't you say?
SAM	Don't know.
HONEY	How could you let Cornwallis treat everybody so badly?
SAM	Don't know. Thought I was doing my job.
HONEY	Doing your job?
SAM	After Lord John and how kind he was, Christopher's behaviour... I've been in shock.
HONEY	I'm not surprised.
SAM	He made all these promises about my career, my future, even said he'd pay me double. And the promises....
HONEY	Came to nothing.
SAM	All lies. All manipulation. I've been so stupid.
HONEY	You're not stupid.

SAM	I was blinded by this suave London gent and his promises of a managerial job in a large care home in London.
HONEY	He promised you what?
SAM	A big job with an even bigger salary. It would be an amazing career move.
HONEY	That's what you want? A big job in London with a flashy car and penthouse flat? You want to be like him?
SAM	That's what I thought. But it's not really me is it?
HONEY	What do you think?
SAM	That I love it here.

Sam edges towards Honey.

HONEY	Hold on a minute. I told you Cornwallis was up to no good and you ignored me.
SAM	True.
HONEY	He fired me and you did nothing.
SAM	True.
HONEY	He's treated everybody so badly and you've let him.
SAM	True.
HONEY	What have you got to say about that?
SAM	I'm a gullible idiot who only saw the truth when it was almost too late. The residents deserve better. You deserve better. I'm so sorry Honey. Do you forgive me.

Honey pauses then takes Sam's hand.

HONEY	Of course I do you idiot.
SAM	You do?
HONEY	You can be so slow to catch on. There's not enough time now. There's lots to do. Let's join the fight for the Beeches. The residents deserve to keep their homes. They just belong here as if they are part of the manor and it's history.
SAM	Thank you. Honey. I want you to know...

HONEY	Yes....yes...what is it?
SAM	We need to go.
HONEY	Sam! You really are the most annoying man I have ever....

Sam exits and Honey follows. Lights down.

SCENE EIGHT

Lights up. Forest Lounge. Half an hour later. Everything is quiet in the lounge as all wait for news from Iris. Cassandra and Walker are still meditating but Colonel has fallen asleep. Iris suddenly jumps up.

IRIS	Eureka!

Everybody jumps out of their skins.

IRIS	What has got into you all. You used to be made of stronger stuff than that.
COLONEL	We were deep in meditation Iris.
WALKER	Communin' with stars.
CASSANDRA	I never thought I'd see the day!
WALKER	I saw night. Total darkness. Awesome.

Walker looks around the room in wonder and verybody is shocked by the change in him.

CASSANDRA	What have you found Iris?
IRIS	In an encrypted file, a right devil to crack open, I found the codicil to his will. Interestingly it was created only a few months ago. Let me read this to you. In the event of Lord John Cornwallis' death, ownership of Beeches Manor Estate will be transferred to Lady Caroline Cornwallis.
WALKER	Not to Cornwallis?
IRIS	No. The usual aristocratic practice is to pass the entire estate to the eldest son but not here.
COLONEL	He has purposefully avoided passing the estate to his son.
IRIS	Indeed.
COLONEL	Not surprised. He's a cad.

CASSANDRA	And The Boss was a true gentleman.
COLONEL	Who clearly didn't trust his son to continue his legacy.
CASSANDRA	But he could trust his wife.
IRIS	Lady C is the owner of Beeches Manor Estate and Cornwallis has been prevented from having control which leads me to my next point...
CASSANDRA	Lady C is in danger.
IRIS	Exactly.
WALKER	'E's capable of anythin'.
IRIS	We need to locate Lady C and keep her safe. I suggest we bring her here. And quickly.

Colonel and Walker bump together as they run about the room.

COLONEL	Quickly. We need to act quickly.
WALKER	Quick. Let's get Lady C?
CASSANDRA	Who's going to do that?
WALKER	*(pointing at Colonel)* It'll have to be us. We're the men for that job.
COLONEL	Do you think? My back's a bit dodgy now.
WALKER	My chest does give me grief.
COLONEL	Where is Lady C anyway?
WALKER	In the manor.
COLONEL	Where in the manor?
WALKER	Don't ask me?
COLONEL	Perhaps in her room?
WALKER	Which of the forty rooms is hers?
COLONEL	Don't ask me!
CASSANDRA	Do you think we need a plan Iris.
IRIS	Indeed.

Iris claps her hands together. Colonel, Walker and Cassandra stand to attention.

COLONEL	Yes General.

IRIS	What has got into all of you. You used to be made of braver stuff.

All look embarrassed at their feet.

IRIS	Here's the plan. Lady C's room is located on the second floor of Main Wing. Take the servants staircase to the second floor, turn right, her room is third on the left. Her room looks out over the gardens and knowing Cornwallis may well be locked. Colonel, you lead the way, Walker you're the expert with lock picking so that's your job, Cassandra you'll be on look out.
WALKER	What will you be doin'?
IRIS	I'm ground control.
WALKER	So you're stayin' here?
IRIS	Yes.
COLONEL	Let's drill this plan to make sure we're all clear. Lead us General.

As Iris sets out the steps of the plan Colonel, Cassandra and Walker act it out in an exaggerated way.

IRIS	Step one - all enter Main Wing of the manor by the west door. Step two - all ascend the servants staircase. Step three - turn right.

Walker turns left and there is chaos.

COLONEL	What are you doing man? Don't you know your left from your right?
WALKER	I went right.
COLONEL	You went left.
WALKER	Right.
COLONEL	So you agree with me.
WALKER	No.
CASSANDRA	Gentlemen I will lead the way.
COLONEL	Good plan.
WALKER	Righto.
COLONEL	Don't start that again.

Iris claps to get their attention. Cassandra leads the way.

IRIS	Step three - turn right. Except Cassandra who will stay at the top of the staircase to keep watch.

Cassandra suddenly stops and turns round. More chaos as they bump into one another.

CASSANDRA	Oops sorry. Turning round.
COLONEL	We turn round?
WALKER	Are you sure?
CASSANDRA	Ouch you're standing on my foot.
COLONEL	Beg your pardon.
IRIS	What has got into all of you? You used to be made of cleverer stuff than this. Step four - proceed to the third room on the left.

All is going well and Colonel and Walker are pleased.

IRIS	Step five - Walker picks the lock to open the door.
WALKER	I don't have my kit? I need it.
COLONEL	Don't be daft man, this is just a rehearsal. You can pick it up in a minute.

Walker acting like a diva.

WALKER	It's no good. I can't practice without the right props.

Cassandra approaches Walker holding out her room key which leads to further chaos.

CASSANDRA	Use this as a prop Walker.
COLONEL	What are you doing here? You're meant to be keeping watch at the top of the staircase.
CASSANDRA	I'm helping Walker.
COLONEL	Well don't. Keep to your post.

Iris claps her hands.

IRIS	Let's get this right. Walker do you have your prop?
WALKER	Yes General.
IRIS	Are you both ready?
COL/W	Yes General.

IRIS	Step five - Walker picks the lock. Step six - Colonel enters the room and finds Lady Cornwallis. Step seven - Colonel talks to Lady Cornwallis and gently leads her away, with Walker's help if necessary...

Colonel picks up an unused coat stand to act in place of Lady C. Walker thinking Iris means the Colonel needs his help grabs the coat stand on the other side. There is a stand off during which Colonel grabs back the coat stand and this results in pushing and shoving.

WALKER	What you doin'?
COLONEL	*(shoving Walker)* This.
WALKER	Well 'ave this.
COLONEL	You have this. I don't need your help.
WALKER	Yes you do Lady C is weak and I need to be on her other side.
COLONEL	Lady C is not weak and has taken my strong arm, which she has admired, and is walking well without your help.
WALKER	No she 'aint.
COLONEL	Yes she is.

Cassandra and Iris look at one another and shake their heads in despair.

IRIS	We need a plan B.
CASSANDRA	Don't you think this ones going to work?
IRIS	Perhaps not.

Iris and Cassandra laugh as Walker and Colonel front up to one another. Lights down.

SCENE NINE

Lights up. Small dark room in the manor house. Following Scene Five. Lady C looks shocked and sits in her chair.

CORNWALLIS	Who's there? How dare you. Get out of my house. Get out now!

George steps out from the shadows into the room.

CORNWALLIS	You're trespassing. Leave.

George touches Lady C's shoulder and they smile at each other.

CORNWALLIS Who are you? What do you want here?

GEORGE I'm here for Lady Caroline.

CORNWALLIS *(laughs)* You're not taking mother anywhere.

GEORGE Let's ask her shall we?

CORNWALLIS Who are you? One moment. Aren't you that new resident?

GEORGE *(to Lady C)* Would you like to leave with me?

CORNWALLIS You're not taking her anywhere.

LADY C Thank you George I would. I knew you'd come.

Cornwallis approaches his mother.

CORNWALLIS George? How you do know this man?

George leads Cornwallis' attention away from Lady C.

GEORGE George Taylor. I would say it's a pleasure to meet you but that would be a lie.

CORNWALLIS Damn you. Get away. Leave her alone.

Cornwallis lunges at George but he easily side steps the attack.

GEORGE Lady Caroline wishes to come with me.

CORNWALLIS You can't just come in here and leave with my mother.

GEORGE *(to Lady C)* Shall I tell him?

LADY C Yes. I've never had the courage.

GEORGE She's my mother too.

Cornwallis is astounded and begins to fall to pieces.

CORNWALLIS What are you talking about. I'm her only son!

LADY C I'm sorry Christopher we should have sat you down and told years ago. In a calm, quiet way, not like this, but I was too weak. I could never crush your spirit like that. You always so loved being the only child, being the centre, knowing it was all about you. I'm so sorry.

CORNWALLIS *(crying)* No mother no, that can't be right. You can't do this to me, you can't. I won't allow it.

Lights down.

SCENE TEN

Lights up. Forest Lounge. The chaos of acting out the plan to save Lady C continues. Colonel and Walker argue, Cassandra and Iris shake their heads waiting for them to see sense.

COLONEL   I'm strong enough to get Lady C on my own.

WALKER   You need my 'elp.

COLONEL   No I don't.

WALKER   She's weak. She needs two of us.

The main doors to the lounge open. Iris and Cassandra notice but not Colonel and Walker. The doors remain open.

COLONEL   Lady C is strong enough to walk back to Forest Lounge with only one person. That person is....

Enter George with Lady C on his arm wrapped in a blanket.

GEORGE   Me!

WALKER   Lady C!

COLONEL   George, you're going to get it now.

Colonel starts to move to attack George but realises he can't without harming Lady C.

COLONEL   Leave her alone.

LADY C   *(calmly)* All is well Colonel. George is my ... good friend.

WALKER   But 'e's the one responsible for us losin' our home.

Lady Caroline and George look bemused.

IRIS   Where did you get that daft idea?

WALKER   We've been discussin' it for weeks, 'e 'as that connection to Newfield Housin'.

IRIS   Oh that? That was so yesterday. Investigations have moved on from that. *(indicating Lady C)* More importantly...

CASSANDRA   More importantly. Lady Cornwallis, please do take a seat.

LADY C   Thank you.

CASSANDRA   How are you?

LADY C   Better now. I have to admit I was a little shaky.

GEORGE	When Lord John became ill Cornwallis found his will leaving the estate to his wife and not his son. To keep tight control over them and the estate Cornwallis shut his parents in one upstairs room in the manor and they have remained there since.
COLONEL	I'll kill him.
LADY C	He is still my son Colonel.
COLONEL	Apologies. I'll only inflict excruciating pain then.

Colonel mimes one of his torture holds.

CASSANDRA	Colonel behave.
GEORGE	Cornwallis plans to sell the house which he knows Lady C would never allow so he's been trying to manipulate her into signing.
COLONEL	I'll....slap his face for him.
IRIS	How did you get Lady C away from Cornwallis?
GEORGE	Money talks Iris and after a short discussion he sold out and let us leave without any bloodshed.
WALKER	How much? How much did you have to pay?
GEORGE	*(looking at Lady C)* I can't say.
LADY C	Don't be shy on my account George. I know my son well. It'll be no surprise to me.
GEORGE	I promised him two million.

All are shocked. Even Lady C.

WALKER	Pounds?
COLONEL	Of course it's pounds. Cornwallis is not going to accept pennies?
WALKER	*(laughs)* Credit where credit is due George, you're a great conman. There's no way you've got two million quid.
GEORGE	If you say so.
WALKER	That's obvious. If you 'ad millions you wouldn't be livin' 'ere.

IRIS	Back to the point. Cornwallis allowed Lady C to leave, just like that?

SCENE ELEVEN

As before. Enter Cornwallis laughing in an evil way.

CORNWALLIS	You didn't think it would be that easy did you George?

Cornwallis pulls out an old second World War pistol and points it around at the residents searching for George.

CORNWALLIS	Think I'm all about the money do you George?
GEORGE	*(confidently)* Yes.
LADY C	Christopher, what are you doing?
CORNWALLIS	Well brother George you're wrong. I like respect too. Respect and the truth and I've been denied them for years. Decades built on lies. And it's all your fault.

All residents are distracted by Cornwallis calling George his brother.

CORNWALLIS	You think you're so clever. This is no fairy story. Bastard son returns in glory to claim his inheritance.

Cornwallis is about to speak again but is interrupted by Iris.

IRIS	*(to George)* George, what precisely is your relationship to him and Lady Cornwallis?
CORNWALLIS	*(laughing)* You don't know? You weren't all in on this?

All stay quiet.

CORNWALLIS	So dear George has kept his dirty little secret quiet all this time mother. Such a great son.
GEORGE	I couldn't say anything. This doesn't just affect me, it would have....
LADY C	What George means is he's Christopher's older brother but not John's son.
IRIS	George is your son?
CASSANDRA	Iris, let Lady Caroline explain.

LADY C   John and I were engaged in the early years of the war. When he was called up I accepted I wouldn't see much of him but then he disappeared, went off the radar for almost a year. No letter, no call, nothing. That was not like John so I convinced myself he must be dead.

CORNWALLIS   Carry on mother, we are all intrigued to hear how this came about.

LADY C   You must understand it was wartime, it wouldn't have happened otherwise, one thoughtless night with an old friend who'd also lost somebody. Then John returns out of the blue. He'd been on top secret manoeuvres and couldn't make contact. Not even with his fiancee. I've always regretted what I put John through but I can't regret my baby.

CASSANDRA   We do understand. Don't upset yourself.

Cornwallis waves the gun around.

CORNWALLIS   Where does it leave me?

LADY C   We'll talk about that. You're still my son.

IRIS   How did Lord Cornwallis react?

LADY C   As you'd expect, a tower of strength. Against all odds, he still wanted us to marry.

CASSANDRA   You were pregnant.

LADY C   Yes. I was keeping out of sight not knowing what the future would be. John only wanted to protect me from scandal, Baby George was born in secret and we gave him to a childless couple on the estate. We married and John continued his war work here at Beeches. Christopher was never told about George for his own peace of mind.

CORNWALLIS   My own peace of mind! What peace of mind! My whole life is based on lies!

LADY C   Christopher calm down. Put the gun away and we can talk about this and sort everything out.

CORNWALLIS   No.

All freeze except Iris.

IRIS   I say, this is a Funny Business. *(aside)* Walker. The Boss.

Iris points to the portrait of Lord John as Colonel approaches Cornwallis who moves beside Lady C.

COLONEL   How dare you wave a gun around. I'll have your....

CORNWALLIS Stay back. I'll shoot.

Cassandra starts to flail her arms around.

CASSANDRA   Your father's energy still fills up this room. It moves and shifts around the whole house....

Walker takes down Lord John's portrait to try and distract Cornwallis.

COLONEL   Lord Cornwallis, what on earth has happened to the portrait of your father, it's disappeared?

WALKER   Is this it over 'ere?

CORNWALLIS Stay back I say. You're pathetic. I'm not falling for this again.

Walker puts the portrait back. George approaches Cornwallis.

CORNWALLIS Keep back I say. Or I will...

Cornwallis halfheartedly puts the gun near Lady C's face but not at her face.

CORNWALLIS You're all going to do as I say or do you want to see my dear mother hurt? Sit down. Now.

All residents sit.

CORNWALLIS Listen to me. This is what's going to happen. George, transfer the money now.

GEORGE   The money's off the table.

CORNWALLIS You weasel. Two million. You promised.

GEORGE   You didn't keep your side of the bargain.

CORNWALLIS Think you're in a position to bargain do you? You'll see. I don't need your lousy money. She is coming with me to sign papers and then I'll be richer than you and shot of this dump and you pathetic idiots.

There is nothing George, Colonel or Walker can do as they fear for Lady C's safety.

LADY C   Christopher please!

CORNWALLIS Please what, mother? I told father years ago not to invite them in here.

LADY C   He owes these people a great deal. We all do.

CORNWALLIS Don't make me laugh. I don't owe them anything. They're good for nothings who've only cluttered up the manor for years.

LADY C   Is that why you never came to see us?

CORNWALLIS I was busy.

LADY C   Too busy to visit your mother and father. John longed to see you, but you always had an excuse.

CORNWALLIS My work is important mother.

LADY C   But your father.

CORNWALLIS My father.The great Lord John Cornwallis. Soft, old fool. Fell for any sob story. Wasted who knows how much on any poor beggar who asked for his help. Frittered everything away on lowlifes whilst this place went to ruin and my inheritance dwindled to nothing.

Colonel is incensed and wants to attack Cornwallis. Cassandra knows this before Colonel does so stops him in his tracks.

LADY C   That is what you think of your father?

CORNWALLIS He never gave me anything. All he cared about was helping other people. Never his own son.

LADY C   He loved you Christopher.

CORNWALLIS No. I deserved better.

LADY C   That's enough!

Lady C puts her head in her hands.

IRIS   More than enough to put you away. Locking your parents in a room for months, preventing your mother from going to her husband's funeral, manipulating her to sign away the estate and now holding us all at gun point.

Cornwallis laughs.

CORNWALLIS She won't press charges. You're coming with me mother. Let's get those papers signed.

LADY C   I will never sign Beeches away!

CORNWALLIS   Pay me my due and I will never return to this hovel. This is my inheritance.

All residents are in shock at what Cornwallis has said. Lady C rises from her chair. She faces Cornwallis and coolly pulls the gun from his hands. All gasp.

LADY C   Get out!

CORNWALLIS   Mother!

LADY C   Ever since you were a child I've tolerated your coldness. Overlooked your dismissive treatment of us and others due to your obsession with money, status, the latest trend. For years I've told myself you would change. But no more. You have shown only contempt for your father and everything he stood for, everything that was good, kind and decent. I want you to leave.

CORNWALLIS   Not without the money.

LADY C   There is no money.

CORNWALLIS   Then I'm not leaving. Not without the money.

LADY C   Colonel?

COLONEL   Yes Lady Cornwallis?

LADY C   Escort my son out of the manor please.

COLONEL   My pleasure. I'll make him pay for all this. Very slowly.

LADY C   No violence Colonel. Agreed?

COLONEL   As you say Ma'am. *(aside)* But it'll be hard not to just...

IRIS   *(to Colonel)* Let it go Colonel. You touch a hair on his head and he'll have you banged up within minutes.

CASSANDRA   He's not worth your freedom. We need you here.

COLONEL   Loud and clear Ladies.

Colonel nods to Walker and they take hold of Cornwallis.

LADY C	I never want to see you again. Find your money elsewhere. Beeches Manor will never pay off your gambling debts.
CORNWALLIS	That's my inheritance Mother. You owe me.
LADY C	After today I owe you nothing. Leave!
CORNWALLIS	Mother, you can't do this. Mother please. I need the money. Soon. They're coming for me. Mother! Mother!
LADY C	Goodbye Christopher.
CORNWALLIS	How could you do this? To your own son. Mother, Mother.....

Colonel and Walker exit with Cornwallis. Lady C collapses back into her chair.

CASSANDRA	Lady Cornwallis!
LADY C	Call me Caroline,
CASSANDRA	Caroline. That was so brave.
LADY C	The hardest thing I've ever had to do.
GEORGE	*(to Lady C)* Taking the gun like that was too dangerous. What were you thinking?
LADY C	The gun was the easy part.
GEORGE	But it could have gone off?
LADY C	Not that old thing. It was John's army gun which he kept in the office.
GEORGE	He had a gun in the house?
LADY C	Decommissioned years ago. He only kept it as a memento of the best team he ever worked alongside.

Lady C smiles at Cassandra and Iris.

GEORGE	So the gun wouldn't have fired?
LADY C	Of course not.
IRIS	But Christopher didn't know that.
LADY C	I'm not sure. I'm choosing to believe he knew it wouldn't work.
CASSANDRA	He's gone now. *(to Lady C)* You're safe, we're all safe and Beeches Manor is safe.

LADY C   Such a relief but I can't be happy.

CASSANDRA   Your son?

LADY C   What will become of him?

Colonel and Walker return.

COLONEL   He's gone Lady Caroline. We watched him head for the gates.

LADY C   Thank you.

Sad pause.

LADY C   I can't say this is what I wanted.

COLONEL   He's behaved appallingly Your Ladyship. He deserves a lot worse.

LADY C   Colonel, please. He's still my son.

WALKER   The Colonel is sayin' that Cornwallis 'as got away with everythin'. Literally walked out of 'ere with no punishment.

CASSANDRA   He will get his karma.

WALKER   Leave 'im to the London 'eavies.

LADY C   How do you know about that?

WALKER   The Boss was no gambler. That left our new Lord in the frame and 'e's been desperately doing everythin' to grab money.

IRIS   Walker, good deduction.

WALKER   You sound surprised.

IRIS   I am. But also impressed.

WALKER   Thanks.

LADY C   George, what will they do to him?

CASSANDRA   Colonel. Don't you say a word. You'll upset Lady Caroline.

COLONEL   I wouldn't dare.

GEORGE   I dread to think what they'll do.

LADY C   He's done wrong. Harmed us all. But I still couldn't bear the thought that he was...

GEORGE	I know. It won't do you any good to think of him suffering like that. I'll visit him in London soon and help him out.
LADY C	You'd pay his debts?
GEORGE	For you.
COLONEL	After everything he's done?
GEORGE	For you yes.
LADY C	Thank you George. You understand me so well.
WALKER	'Old on a minute. You're tellin' us that you can pay off all Cornwallis' debts just like that?
GEORGE	Yes.
IRIS	I have a question George, if you don't mind?
GEORGE	You'll ask whatever I say, so fire away.

Sharp intake of breath from everybody.

GEORGE	Sorry, not a good choice of words.
IRIS	What's your real name?
GEORGE	George Taylor.
WALKER	I knew 'e wasn't a Lowe.
GEORGE	I had to hide my identity.
IRIS	George Taylor? I know that name. Got it! You're that multi-millionaire tech owner!
WALKER	No 'e's not.
IRIS	Yes he is.
WALKER	'E's no multi-millionaire. Look at 'im.
GEORGE	I can confirm that I recently sold my share in Twycon Ltd for eighty million pounds.
COLONEL	Hold on, I saw an article about that acquisition in the paper. That's you?
GEORGE	That's me.
CASSANDRA	I always knew you had hidden depths.
GEORGE	No you didn't.
CASSANDRA	I did I saw a golden hue in your aura.
GEORGE	Poppycock.

IRIS	George is an extremely wealthy man Walker.
WALKER	Then what's 'e been doing 'ere?
IRIS	Work it out.

While Walker thinks George explains.

GEORGE	Knowing that Lord Cornwallis was very ill I wanted to keep a close eye on him and his wife. I told you that I didn't trust Christopher Cornwallis. When the opportunity came up to take Cecil's room I grabbed it.
WALKER	You've made fools of us all.
GEORGE	That wasn't the intention. I had to keep my identity secret from Christopher Cornwallis. If I remember correctly you thought I was the fool.

Colonel and Walker clear their throats in embarrassment.

COLONEL	Sorry old chap.
WALKER	We got it wrong.
GEORGE	Cornwallis is now out of the picture. I can secure the future of Beeches Manor Estate and will run it on behalf of Lady Cornwallis. That is less than I owe Lord John. He always supported me and my adopted family and afforded me the best education money could buy. I am so grateful to be in a position to be able to repay that kindness in this small way.
IRIS	To The Boss.

Residents (except George) line up one by one, face the portrait, place one arm across their chest and bow their heads.

ALL	The Boss.
GEORGE	Might I ask you a question Iris?
IRIS	Yes do.
GEORGE	What is the connection between this house and you all?
IRIS	Nothing.
CASSANDRA	It's not important George.
COLONEL	Forget it.
GEORGE	The Boss?

WALKER	We all look up to him.
GEORGE	That's all?
WALKER	Yup.
GEORGE	I don't get it.
LADY C	It's something that is kept from you for your own sake. It's to do with a team John would never forget and promised to take care of as long as he was able.
GEORGE	Surely you can tell me now.
LADY C	I can't. Top secret. Let's just say the specialist code work done at Beeches in Alan's words "saved thousands of lives".
GEORGE	You don't mean Alan Turing?
LADY C	I couldn't possibly answer that enigma.
GEORGE	Not another one of Iris' crossword clues?
IRIS	Could be? I couldn't possibly say. Do you have any other surprises for us today George?
GEORGE	There is one more. Not even Lady Cornwallis. knows about this.
CASSANDRA	I had a feeling there was more.
COLONEL	We'll need a few days to recover from all this.
LADY C	Tell us then George. We've had enough suspense for one day.
GEORGE	I've bought a major share in Newfield Housing so that they will never develop this site.
LADY C	George, how humbling. Thank you.
WALKER	What a deal! Take my 'at off to you George... Taylor.
COLONEL	I underestimated you old chap.
IRIS	You're a marvel George.
CASSANDRA	And one of us now.
LADY C	He is a marvel and my saviour.
GEORGE	Thank you. Mother. Might I call you that in public?

LADY C	Of course my son. Welcome to this Beeches family.
ALL	Welcome George!
LADY C	If only my other son could be part of this too.
CASSANDRA	He'll move through this.
LADY C	If he survives.
CASSANDRA	He's a Cornwallis. He's strong. He'll survive and one day he will find his heart.
LADY C	I'm not so sure.
CASSANDRA	He will. Until then, here's to Lady Cornwallis.
ALL	Lady Cornwallis!

Honey and Sam enter and do not see Lady C.

SAM	Have we missed something?

Everybody laughs except Sam and Honey.

HONEY	We have missed something.
SAM	What's going on?
WALKER	You tell us what's been goin' on between you.
CASSANDRA	I feel news in the air.
HONEY	Shall I tell them?
SAM	Yes. You tell them.

Honey waves her engagement ring in the air.

HONEY	We're engaged!
SAM	Have been for the past hour.
WALKER	Way hay!

Cassandra pushes Walker out of the way.

CASSANDRA	What lovely news.
IRIS	The best.
COLONEL	Well done you two.
WALKER	Do you know what this calls for...

Everybody is very nervous about what Walker is going to say as he makes his way to another hidden stash.

WALKER	Champagne. This is a double celebration.

Residents find champagne glasses in hidden places.

SAM	A double celebration. What else are we celebrating?
GEORGE	Nothing much, we can tell you later.
HONEY	Lady Cornwallis. How lovely to see you. Are you well?
LADY C	Iris would say I am a day without rain.

All look blank.

HONEY	Sunny?
SAM	Dry?
WALKER	Sober?
COLONEL	Dusty?

Iris shoots Colonel a withering look.

IRIS	She's fine everybody. Lady Cornwallis is fine.

Everybody is relieved.

GEORGE	Let's make a toast. To Beeches Manor!
ALL	To Beeches Manor.

Lights down. Sound of champagne corks and congratulations.

Printed in Great Britain
by Amazon